W9-BUG-980

$500 room makeovers

clarkson potter/publishers
new york

photographs by matthew carden

LISA QUINN

$500 room make-overs

Copyright © 2006 by Lisa Quinn
Photographs copyright © 2006
by Matthew Carden

All rights reserved.
Published by Clarkson Potter/Publishers, an imprint
of the Crown Publishing Group, a division of
Random House, Inc., New York.
www.crownpublishing.com
www.clarksonpotter.com

Clarkson N. Potter is a trademark and
Potter and colophon are registered
trademarks of Random House, Inc.

Library of Congress Cataloging-in-Publication
Data
Quinn, Lisa.
$500 room makeovers / Lisa Quinn;
photographs by Matthew Carden.—1st ed.
Includes index.
1. Interior decoration—Handbooks, manuals, etc.
2. Interior decoration accessories.   I. Title: Five
hundred dollar room makeovers.   II. Title.
NK2115.Q56   2006
747'.883—dc22   2005006992

ISBN-13: 978-1-4000-9779-1
ISBN-10: 1-4000-9779-7

Printed in China

Design by Jan Derevjanik

10 9 8 7 6 5 4 3 2 1

First Edition

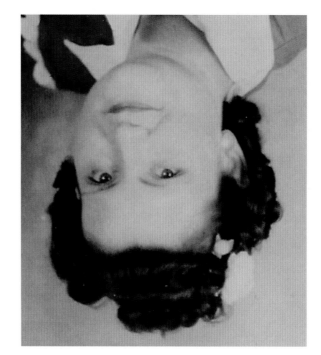

To Jettie May,
I only wish you could have
been here to see this.

acknowledgments

I would like to take this opportunity to thank the village of people who kept me from looking like an idiot through the whole process of making this book. You are all just wonderful and I could never have done it without you.

Kristy Savicke—Your keen vision and ferocious tenacity are responsible for this project taking flight. Thank you so much for believing in me.

Matthew Carden—For your incredible photographs and for going above and beyond the call of duty on so many occasions. You are a multitalented artist, a patient colleague, and a true friend.

Lena Sullivan and Chris Bollini (aka Mistress and Master of the Billy Bookcase)—For your creative input, never-ending support, and loads of belly laughs.

Michael O'Rourke, Katie Quartey, and the truly awesome staff at IKEA Emeryville—Michael, thank you so much for taking a crazy chance on me.

Vivianna Coriat, Nin Assi, and the equally awesome staff at IKEA East Palo Alto—You saved me in my many times of need. I'm proud to call you colleagues and friends.

My editors at Clarkson Potter, Christopher Pavone and Aliza Fogelson—For your sage advice and saint-like patience.

Jan Derevjanik, Marysarah Quinn, Sibylle Kazeroid, and Felix Gregorio—You amaze me. I send in a mess of papers and disks and I end up with this fabulous book. You guys rock.

Greg Morgan (aka the Hardest-Working Man in Show Business) and all the generous folks at Kelly Moore Paint—Greg, you have no idea how many times your consummate professionalism and quick wit eased my worried mind.

Jon Stone and the crew from Brescia-Stone Painting Inc.—Thank you for consistently doing such an amazing job and never complaining that we were *always* late.

Dr. JLo., Jessica Winchell Morsa, and Juli Fields—For your constant encouragement and steadfast friendship.

My family—For your unconditional love and support, and for listening patiently every time I went on and on and on about this book.

Michael—For everything you do. You are the sweetest, smartest, funniest, most supportive man I've ever known (and the second most handsome). My heart was wrapped up in clover the night I looked at you. . . .

And finally, to all the homeowners who so graciously let us barrel in and completely take over their homes for three days. Your hospitality and open-mindedness were much appreciated. I hope we did you proud.

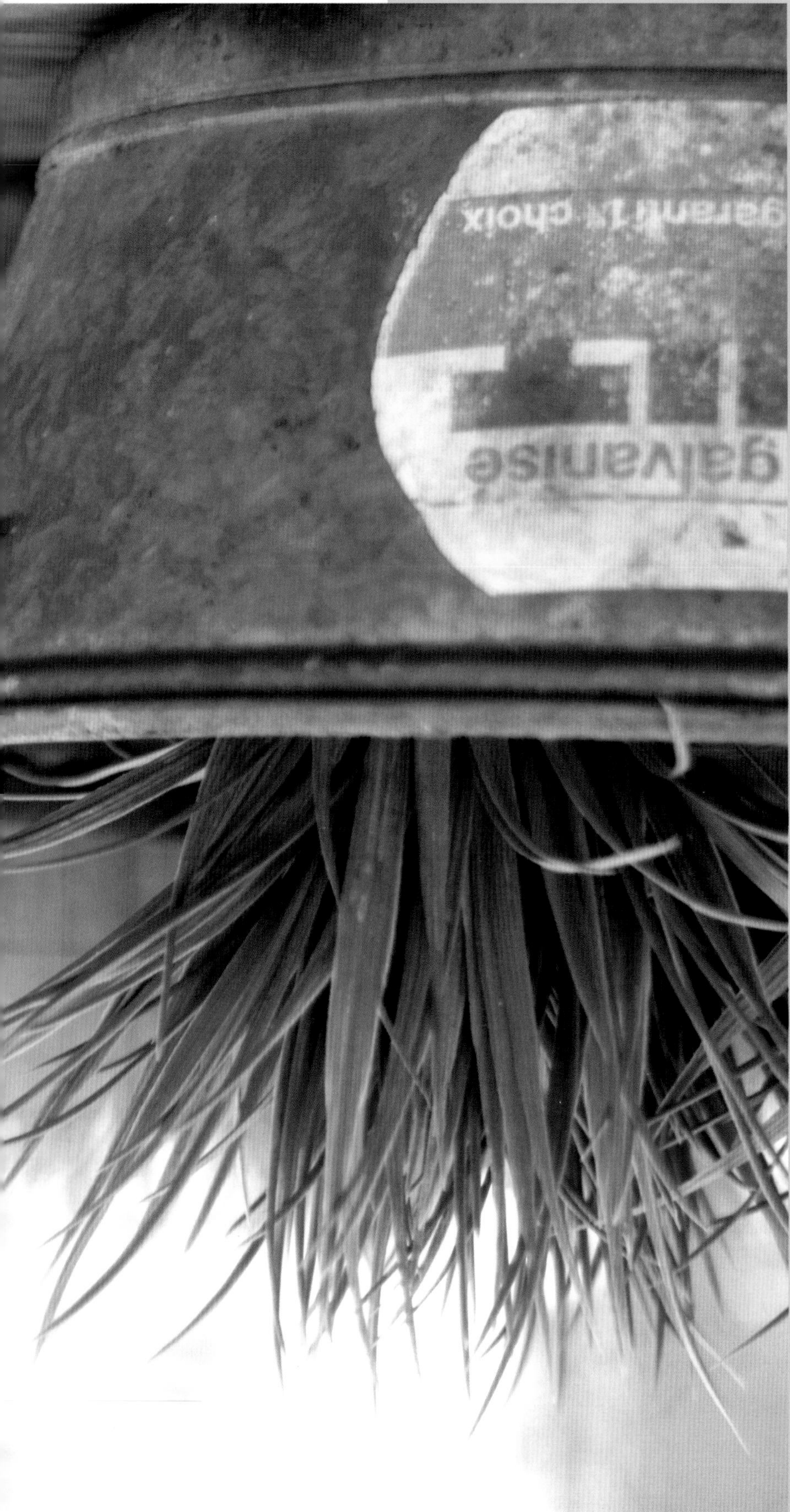
garanti 1er choix
galvanisé

contents

Introduction   9

dramatic rooms   11
Sexy Bedroom   12
Surfer Chic Lounge   20
Moulin Rouge Studio   28
Feminine Dining Room   36
Gothic Bedroom   44
Pop Art Bedroom   52

classic rooms   61
Botanical Dining Room   62
Peaceful Bedroom   70
Floral Workspace   78
Jade Living Room   86
Luxe Patio   94
Contemporary Dining Room   102

exotic rooms   111
Moroccan Den   112
Mexican Living Room   120
African Lounge   128
Asian Retreat   136
Pad Thai   144

children's rooms   153
Pretty in Pink Nursery   154
Cowpoke Nursery   162
C Is for Cole   170
Flower Power   178

Resources   187
Index   189

introduction

It all started with the squashes . . .

When I was a child, my grandmother was a huge influence on me. Born with a creative streak a mile wide and raised in rural Mississippi during the Depression, she honed a remarkable talent for seeing the unlimited possibilities in ordinary objects. Any given day might find us defending a fortress constructed from apple crates or riding shotgun on ponies rustled from the broom closet. But my all-time favorite activity was the squash dolls: After a morning at the farmer's market, we would rescue a few squashes destined for the stewpot and construct these outrageously flamboyant dolls. Anything pillaged from the scrap basket was fair game: buttons, earrings, feathers. If she had the time, my grandmother would even tailor the latest in "squash fashion" while watching her afternoon "stories" on the television. Not only were these playthings less expensive than my store-bought toys, but they were also more fun because we'd made them together. My goal with this book is to carry on the enterprising spirit Mamaw planted in me.

That spirit was put to the test with my first apartment. Hand-me-downs and thrift-store finds were all I could afford. But I refused to accept my fate, and I discovered clever ways to get the biggest bang for my buck. Some ideas were practical, like using inexpensive tablecloths to disguise that my dining table was actually a cable spool. Other ideas didn't fare as well—friends still laugh about the sofa I tried to spray-paint (it seemed like a reasonable plan at the time).

My enthusiasm for decorating eventually led to a career in interior design. I quickly learned there's a lot of fear and loathing out there concerning home decoration. In fact, many people are too full of dread to even start the process. And the ones who *do* take action are often tethered by the perceived expense, afraid to step outside the boundaries of cookie-cutter decor. I believe that living in a home that doesn't reflect your personal style is like wearing someone else's shoes: They may do the job, but they will never feel right. This dissatisfaction can lead to one remodel after another and be very expensive in the end. I say go easy on the wallet until you're more certain of your individual style. In the meantime, take some chances while the investment is small. As you become more confident, you can build on this foundation. Eventually, you can create a home that truly represents you, and the things you love.

I am a firm believer in simplicity. Who has time for labor-intensive projects? I do this for a *living*, and I can barely find the time myself. My approach is to keep the game plan uncomplicated and, whenever possible, to repurpose everyday household items. In these pages, you will discover an old door and a few baskets converted into a buffet; a pot rack reincarnated as a headboard; and a window treatment created entirely from Burger King crowns (I surprised even myself with that one).

I will try to teach you what my grandmother taught me: Think creatively, have fun, and make the most of what you've got. Don't think of a budget as a restriction. Consider it a challenge; a challenge you can easily master if you just look at things differently.

dramatic rooms

Even the most timid of us have little drama queens inside, demanding a debut. Expressing yourself with bold colors and saucy patterns is a sure way to set your wild side free. These rooms are all different but share the same brazen spirit. If you have the desire to shake things up a little in your home, try these simple tips:

- "HIGH CONTRAST = HIGH DRAMA": Pick colors for your room that have a lot of contrast. When everything has the same intensity of color, it has a calming effect. We want excitement!

- ADD A LITTLE SHIMMER: Gold and silver accents add punch.

- ANIMAL PRINTS ARE ALWAYS IN STYLE; I don't care what anybody says.

- COLOR, COLOR, COLOR!

- A LITTLE TOO SHY TO GO HOG-WILD IN AN ENTIRE ROOM? Go bold in a powder room or dressing area. It's like wearing a black lace camisole under a starched white shirt.

sexy bedroom

BEDROOMS ARE THE PERFECT PLACE TO SET THE MOOD WITH DESIGN CHOICES. To define your mood, establish how you use the room. Obviously, you will be sleeping here. But what other activities will go on in the bedroom? Do you like to read, write, watch TV, or exercise? Will you be *entertaining*? Whatever your activities, it's nice to surround yourself with the things that make you comfortable and ease your mind.

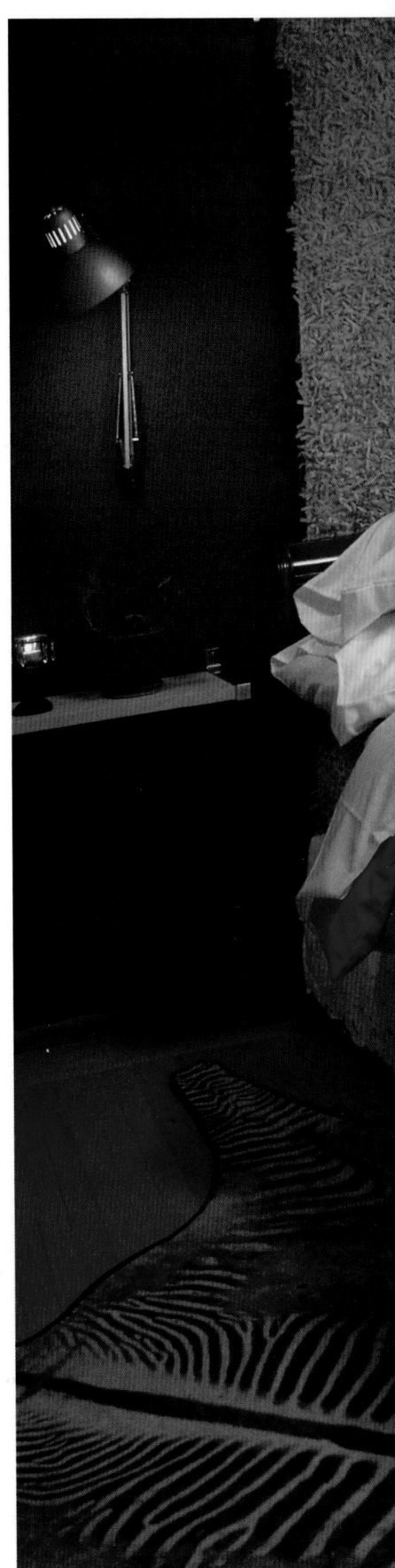

- SET THE MOOD. Candlelight adds instant romance; it can calm you down after a stressful day, and everyone looks more attractive in its warm glow.

- LIGHT UP YOUR LIFE. Make sure you have adequate lighting to read. Picture lights, available at any lighting store, are the small lamps attached to paintings to focus light on the artwork. They make a handy reading light if attached to the back of your headboard.

- LIKE TO SLEEP LATE? Choose blackout curtains to keep the sun at bay. Most home stores offer blackout liners to place behind your existing draperies.

the dilemma

Melissa needs some excitement in the bedroom. Not *that* kind of excitement—it's actually her *room* that needs to see some action. Melissa would like to see her boudoir, currently a mass of mismatched furniture and general disorder, given a flirtatious, dramatic look to suit her personality. She loves her bed and her chaise, which were purchased with this theme in mind. However, since her move-in more than five years ago, she admits to having accumulated more clutter than a distinct style. Melissa has also mentioned a need for tranquillity in the room; something she lacks now with all the disarray—and all the home-office accoutrements that dominate the room. A fan of everything animal print, she wants jaws to drop when people see her room for the first time.

THE GOOD NEWS

- Hardwood floors in good shape are a designer's friend.
- There is an expanse of open wall space, which means more room to hang accessories.
- The chaise, the dresser, and the bed are in good shape and can stay in the room, so more of our budget can go for drama.

THE BAD NEWS

- The room is rather small.
- The only window is an odd shape and is so high it gives the room the feeling of being in a basement.
- The plain white walls are more drab than dramatic.
- Who could relax with so much clutter?

AFTER

BEFORE

THE PLAN

I need to beg Melissa to let me move her office equipment to another area of the home (there's room, I've checked). A bedroom needs to be just that. She will never find tranquillity with fax machines and printers going off at any moment. The wall color will change to a more provocative hue, and the lighting will be more interesting. My goal is to give this disheveled bedroom a sexy makeover with lots of texture and mood for less than $500.

THE GRAND TOTAL: $450.90

the color palette

For Melissa's bedroom, I wanted the drama of black walls. However, considering the small amount of natural light available, I also didn't want it to feel like a cave. The compromise? An "accent wall": We applied a crisp, taupe finish to three of the walls, and then the back wall alone was painted the darkest of charcoal gray. The result is a fabulous focal point and lots of contrast. The spice comes with the bedding: a scarlet-hued duvet cover that demands your attention. Subtle animal accents add to the seduction.

PAINT COLORS

Accent wall: The Edge, Kelly-Moore KM3800-5
Walls: Westover Hills, Kelly-Moore KM3973-2

NEW USES: RUG HEADBOARDS

A creative way to add a little drama to a bed is to extend the height of the headboard by hanging something above it. For this room, I chose a soft, suede shag rug to complement the tactile mood of the space. Nearly any bedroom can benefit from this treatment. If you have a taste for the Southwest, hang a Navajo rug over your bed. Prefer a more traditional look? Hang a Tibetan wool rug and match your bedding to one of the rich jewel tones of the carpet. And you don't have to stop at rugs: Shower curtains come in a variety of fun and edgy designs these days.

SWEET RETREAT

Your bedroom, a place for rest and relaxation, should be the most peaceful spot in your home. Nothing puts a monkey wrench in those works more than having a home office in there with you. Scattered papers, printers, and fax machines . . . How can you get your mind off work when it's right there, mocking you while you try to sleep?

If you find yourself in this predicament, I have a few suggestions. If at all possible, move that office equipment out of your bedroom like we did here. The kitchen, the dining room, the guest room, and the garage are much better suited for the grindstone. If your home is square-footage-challenged and you have no other option, consider an armoire or wardrobe to disguise the workstation. Many furniture stores now offer computer cabinets made specifically for this purpose, ranging in price from $250 to $2,500.

I have even transformed a bedroom closet into an office. If you can spare the storage, place your file cabinets and a shallow desk or a sofa table into your closet, creating an office that you can shut at night.

the details

I introduced luxurious textures to add to the sensual feel—this headboard is actually a suede rug. (For details on how we hung it, check out page 19.)

A customized monogrammed pillow adds a touch of sophistication. (See how I made it on page 18.)

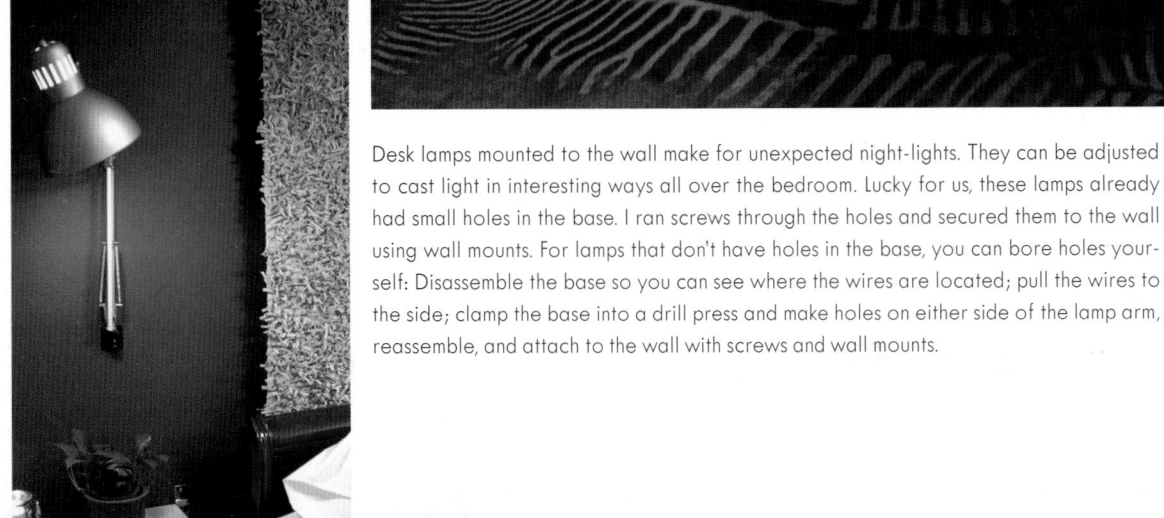

Desk lamps mounted to the wall make for unexpected night-lights. They can be adjusted to cast light in interesting ways all over the bedroom. Lucky for us, these lamps already had small holes in the base. I ran screws through the holes and secured them to the wall using wall mounts. For lamps that don't have holes in the base, you can bore holes yourself: Disassemble the base so you can see where the wires are located; pull the wires to the side; clamp the base into a drill press and make holes on either side of the lamp arm, reassemble, and attach to the wall with screws and wall mounts.

Nothing says "sexy bedroom" like a bawdy red bed. The color choice defines the bed as the focal point in the room. And the zebra rug underneath the bed was purchased for a steal ($115) on eBay.

Removing the home office opened up a corner for a cozy reading nook. Now Melissa can finally relax in her bedroom.

Everyday bookshelves make handsome night tables when storage is not an issue. I paired these wooden shelves with modern stainless-steel hardware for a sleek look. We used a stud finder to locate the studs in the wall, and wood screws to secure the shelves to the wall.

the projects

MONOGRAMMED PILLOW

To keep balance in this bedroom, I chose to mix dark and light colors, bold and calm patterns, and soft and hard textures. I wanted to carry this theme to the bedding as well. The red duvet needed something a bit more tame to keep the design in check (there's a fine line between a sexy bedroom and a bordello!). To give the bed a crisp look, I added white sheets and pillowcases. To top it off, I made a monogrammed pillow.

Items you will need:

Fabric trim

Scissors

Hem tape (this is an iron-on adhesive found at any fabric store)

Throw pillow with removable cover

Iron

Iron-on letter(s)

Here's how you do it:

1. Cut the fabric trim to size with the scissors.

2. Using the hem tape, iron the trim in place on the pillow. It may take a few passes with the iron to firmly secure your trim.

3. Peel the paper backing off the letter(s) and iron in place on the pillow. Done!

AREA RUG HEADBOARD

The bed is usually the most expensive purchase in a bedroom. In our case, we already had a bed, but it was a little boring. I wanted to jazz it up, so I decided to make an easy, inexpensive headboard with drapery clips, which can be found in most home stores. They make it a cinch to hang just about anything from a curtain rod.

Items you will need:

Tape measure

Pencil

Wall mounts and screws (this rug is heavy, so you want to make sure it is fastened securely to the wall; ask someone at the hardware store to help you pick out the right wall mounts for the job)

Screwdriver

Curtain rod

Drapery clips

Rug about the same width as your bed

Here's how you do it:

1. First, measure the height at which you want to hang the curtain rod, making sure to center it over your bed as well. Hang the rod at least 4 inches above that mark, and you will easily clear the rod while seated in bed.

2. Next, mount the wall brackets.

3. Place the drapery clips onto the curtain rod.

4. Clip the rug onto the rod.

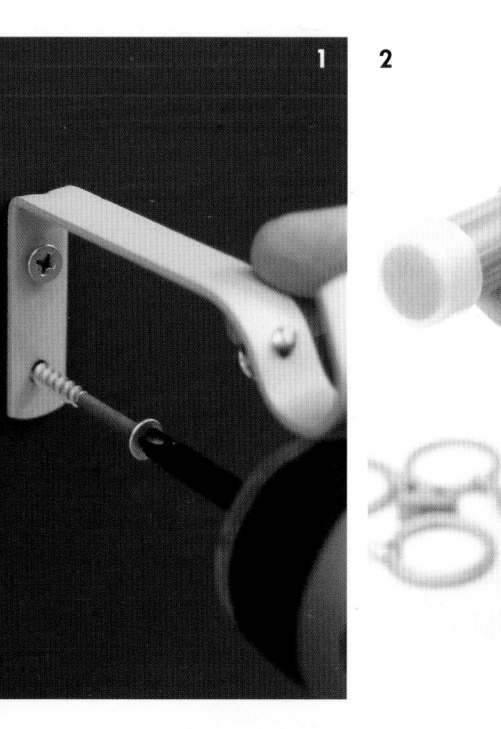

1

2

surfer chic lounge

WHEN YOU WORK FROM HOME, IT'S A MUST TO HAVE A SPACE YOU CAN truly call your workstation: an area with no distractions, proper storage, and adequate lighting; a place where you can sit down and get to work. Here are a few tips for getting professional in your own home:

- CLAIM YOUR SPACE. If square footage is at a minimum and you must share spaces, set up shop in a quiet, permanent location like a guest bedroom or a garage. The distraction of domestic activities can be too tempting when trying to work in areas like the kitchen or den.

- MAKE STORAGE KEY. Shuffling paperwork from one makeshift area to another will keep you disorganized and behind on your work. Most office-supply stores have trained professionals who can help you with storage solutions and design an office where everything is at your fingertips.

- SET THE MOOD. If music makes you more productive, invest in a stereo system. Lighting is another important component in an office, and the overhead bulb is usually not enough. Desk lamps and task lighting can make the difference. If you live in the city, traffic and construction noises may drive you to distraction. Invest in a white noise machine or high-quality headphones.

the dilemma

Mark is an actor, a musician, and a surfer. He's looking for a home office where he can learn his lines, practice his guitar, and catch up on the latest surfer mags. He and his wife have a charming cottage on a hill with stunning city views. They would like to see this lower-level storage area turned into both a funky studio for Mark and a guest room for visitors. They love the comfortable leather chair and ottoman, but are willing to part with the plastic storage bins and the faded cotton rug.

THE GOOD NEWS

- At 19 by 19 feet the area is certainly large enough to accommodate both guest room and office furnishings.
- The leather chair and ottoman are in terrific shape, and their classic lines will work well with any design.
- The neutral low-pile carpeting, while not the most stylish, is clean and unobtrusive.

THE BAD NEWS

- The chair and ottoman are the only pieces of salvageable furniture.
- The fireplace is unattractive and dingy.
- There are no artificial light sources, which are needed for a workspace.

THE PLAN

First, we'll move the unused books, papers, and record albums to a storage area in the garage. This room needs to be a relaxing, inspirational place for Mark to work, and his clutter is distracting. Next, we'll introduce the bright, warm colors of summer to this drab, gray space using paint and accessories. The fireplace will get a face-lift, and the whole dingy area will be transformed into a surfer cowboy lounge—for less than $500.

THE GRAND TOTAL: $494.70

AFTER

BEFORE

NEW USES: **MOUSE PADS**

I needed a cheap quick fix for the artwork in the room, because most of my budget had already been spent on the sleeper sofa (honestly, I had about $8 to spend for an entire wall of art). Necessity being the mother of invention and all, I produced my own art from the office department at IKEA. I will call this piece "Ode to a Mouse Pad," because that's what it's made of: sixteen mouse pads affixed to the wall with finishing nails in a graphic, modern shape. They make a bold statement in this room and, at 50 cents each, I even hit my budget.

But don't stop at office supplies. Take this basic concept and let your imagination fill in the blanks. As long as the individual pieces are similar in shape and size, any item will give you a comparable look. Imagine a wall of vintage pot holders in a sleek, modern kitchen. Hubcaps, place mats, record albums (remember those?), or even drink coasters could also be used for a spectacular effect.

the color palette

This home office is atypical in that our worker bee is an actor, so regular office work will not be a part of the environment. I wanted this space to have a funky, avant-garde feel; to be a place where Mark could feel inspired and creative. The color scheme came from his collection of vintage Hawaiian postcards, the colors of the sea and sun. Celadon green walls with punches of blazing orange accessories make for an exciting, youthful look. Black, white, and silver accents add sophistication.

PAINT COLOR
Alligator Alley, Kelly-Moore KM 3390-2

FIREPLACES

A cozy fireplace aglow in rich, flickering light can be the most soothing, relaxing element in any room. But take a look at the same fireplace in July, and you may be singing a different tune. In the warmer months, fireplaces can look dusty and dark. You can make the most of yours by replacing the heavy iron accessories of winter with softer, more organic elements. In our surfer lounge, I decided to fill the space with firewood that I found right outside the back door. It was certainly the least expensive option, but cost was not the only reason for my choice. I love to place opposites together. The juxtaposition of the rustic wood against the sleek steel adds interest to what was a drab area. Potted plants, antique copper kettles, and candles are also excellent options for lighting a spark in your summertime fireplace.

the details

The brick fireplace got a shiny new makeover. (Learn how to do it yourself on page 26.)

We added some gnarly beach vibe to ordinary table lamps. (See how it was done on page 27.)

Since most of Mark's work involves reading and rehearsing, a proper desk wasn't necessary. I substituted a much less expensive sofa table (also called a console table) in lieu of a more costly office desk.

The best buy in the room was definitely the coffee table. It was being discontinued, and the price had been reduced to $27! Ask your favorite stores when their end-of-the-season and restocking sales occur to score some outrageous deals.

We moved the existing chair and ottoman to the corner of the room and added a floor lamp for a soft glow by which to read. The oblong shape of the lamp mimics that of a surfboard and adds a punch of personality.

The base of our new sofa has the same dimensions as a twin mattress, which means Mark can dress it with standard bed linens for instant guest accommodations. The artwork in the background was fashioned from something you may use in your office every day. (To get the 411, check out page 22.)

the projects

FIREPLACE COVER

I'd always wanted to work with corrugated steel but had never found the right project until here. As a fireplace cover for our beach-inspired office space, it adds a certain surf shack ambience.

Items you will need:

Corrugated steel (enough to cover the area)

Measuring tape

Sharpie or marking pen

Newspaper (optional)

Straightedge

C-clamps

Circular saw with a special metal-cutting blade

Leather gloves

Eye and ear protection

Caulk gun and masonry adhesive caulk

Here's how you do it:

1. Measure and mark the steel to cover the area. (A template made from newspaper can be helpful in this process.) Use the straightedge to ensure that your lines are perfectly level.

2. Secure the metal sheeting to a work surface using the C-clamps. Using the circular saw with a metal-cutting blade, cut out the fireplace cover. This is a loud, violent process; sparks will be flying all over the place, and the saw can get away from you if you're not careful. Remember: "Slow and steady wins the race." Take your time, wear your safety equipment, and all should go fine.

3. Using the caulk gun, apply the masonry adhesive caulk to the "hills" of your corrugated steel. Place the steel against the brick of the fireplace front and secure until dry.

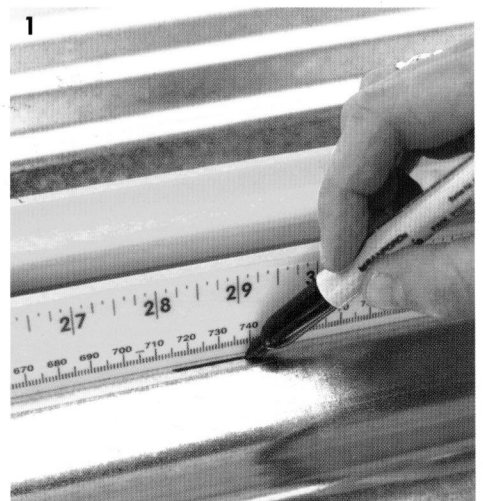

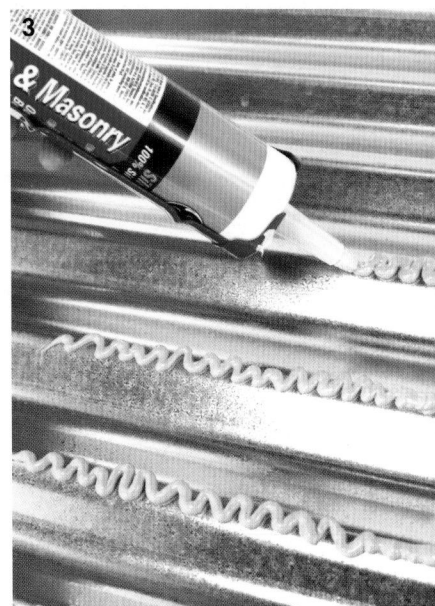

HAWAIIAN LAMP SHADE

Mark owns an impressive collection of vintage Hawaiian postcards. I wanted to incorporate them into his office but wasn't sure how until I purchased the lamps for his desk. The lamps were attractive but needed a bit of pizzazz, so I decided to apply the images to the lamp shades for a touch of island flare.

Items you will need:

Postcards

Photocopier

Scissors

Lamp with shade

Decoupage glue

Artist's brush(es)

Adult-sized hula skirt

Hot-glue gun and glue sticks

Upholstery trim

Here's how you do it:

1. So you can keep the original postcards in their pristine condition, make color copies and cut them out with the scissors. (The lighter weight of the copied images is also much easier to adhere to the rounded surface of the lamp shade.) Apply the images to the lamp shade using the decoupage glue and the artist's brush. But be sure to test the glue on the image first—some copier inks will bleed upon contact with the glue and ruin your project.

2. Next, attach the hula skirt to the bottom edge of the shade using the hot glue. Upholstery trim finishes the look.

3. Trim the skirt to the desired length.

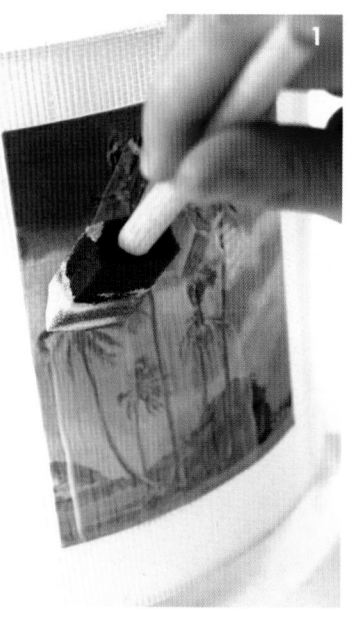

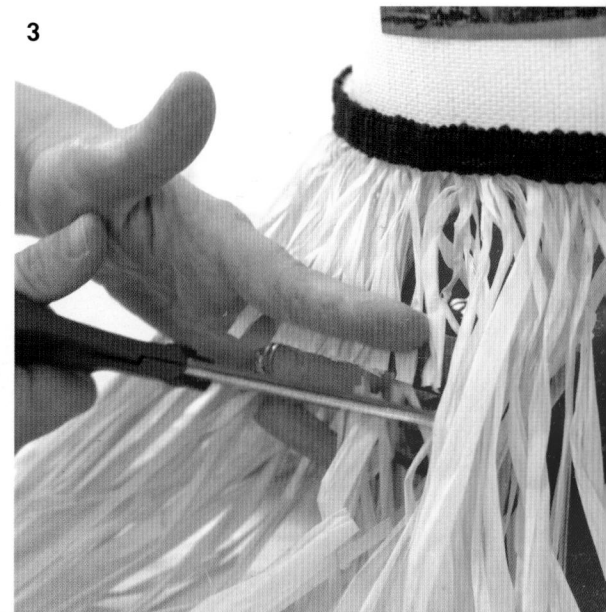

moulin rouge studio

A STUDIO OR AN EFFICIENCY APARTMENT CAN PRESENT A REAL CHALLENGE to the occupant who wants it all. To create a livable space in such a small area, sacrifices must be made. The most difficult decision is usually whether to make this one room appear to be a living room or a bedroom. Do your homework about how you will be using your space before you make any large purchases, because if you change your mind midstream, there will be no room for mistakes.

- DECIDE HOW YOU LIVE. Futons and convertible sofas can give you the best of both worlds in a studio. But the twice-daily grind of folding and unfolding is a hassle. Be honest with yourself about your willingness to take on this task. You don't want your entire apartment looking like an unmade bed every day.

- ORGANIZATION IS KEY FOR A HAPPY STUDIO HOME. Never was the proverb "A place for everything and everything in its place" more relevant. Visit container stores or the organization department of your superstore for storage solutions.

- CONSIDER MULTIPURPOSE FURNISHINGS. A desk that can morph into a dining table or an ottoman with inner storage will be invaluable to the studio resident.

- BE GRATEFUL. The benefit of having a small space is that if you make the right decisions initially, then you won't have to buy as much stuff and, subsequently, you can spend more money on individual items—you'll have all the swank without breaking the bank.

the dilemma

Homeowner Melanie Brenner gave me a real challenge: "Make my studio apartment look like Satine's boudoir in the movie *Moulin Rouge*." I felt a little nervous until I rented the movie; then I felt *extremely* nervous. The bedroom of our heroine is bedecked in a sea of lavish red velvets, silks, and vintage tapestries. Antique crystal chandeliers, multitudes of flickering candles, and a dazzling starlit sky illuminate the space with surreal, dreamlike results. And here I sit with $500. . . . Concessions will certainly need to be made to knock off the look of a multimillion-dollar Hollywood production on the budget of a cable access show. But I know I can can do it. (Get it? *Cancan*? Sorry, I'll stick to the decorating.)

THE GOOD NEWS

- This is a rather large studio (17 by 23 feet).
- The hardwood floors are in excellent shape; I won't have to spend any money on floor coverings.
- There is a huge walk-in closet, so storage is not an issue.
- Intricate, Victorian crown moldings are a big plus when designing this look.

THE BAD NEWS

- There are hardly any furnishings in here to use as a base.
- There is no headboard on the bed.
- This apartment is on the fifth floor, and there is no elevator (okay, that's just bad news to Melanie and me).

AFTER

BEFORE

THE PLAN

I would like to introduce a variety of paint techniques to replicate the lush look of the expensive silk wall coverings from Melanie's favorite movie. The bed needs a headboard to define it as the main focal point in the room, and Melanie needs a dining area for eating and bill paying. My goal is to turn this humble studio into a scene from the movie *Moulin Rouge* for less than $500.

THE GRAND TOTAL: $475.89

the color palette

After watching the movie, it became obvious that I was going to need a lot of red paint. Everything in this character's bedroom is some shade of red: scarlet, ruby, auburn, crimson, and russet tones fill the space. For the studio, I chose two reddish shades in slightly differing hues and intensities. First, the lighter, more golden hue was painted on the walls. Next, the deeper red tone was added to the walls using a decorative stamp to add texture. Ornate crown moldings received an extra shot of glamour with a coat of metallic gold acrylic. A starry sky was painted on the ceiling to replicate the dramatic nighttime sky. (See details on this painting process on page 35.)

PAINT COLORS

Ceiling base color: Connecticut Yankee, Kelly-Moore AC46-N
Ceiling rag roll coat: Diplomat Blue, Kelly-Moore AC51-N
Stars: Acrylic White, Delta Ceramcoat
Trim detail: Acrylic Gold, Delta Ceramcoat
Coved ceiling and stamp color: Christmas Red, Kelly-Moore AC 21-R
Walls: Nuovo, Kelly-Moore AC10-Y

GILDING THE LILY

There's a phrase in interior design that was a guiding force in the making of our *Moulin Rouge* studio: "Gilding the lily" refers to the "more is more" philosophy, or what I like to call Chez Zsa Zsa. Why stop at a Baroque carved mantelpiece when you can gold-leaf it and hang a crystal-beaded garland from the top? Here are some instances where we could not leave well enough alone; we had to make it *fabulous, dahlink*!

The simple, iron wall sconces I purchased for the room needed a lift. I added crystal prisms (purchased on eBay for a steal) using a silicone adhesive. Do not use a hot-glue gun as your adhesive—the heat from the lightbulbs will melt the glue, and all of your crystals will fall off like so many snowflakes. Trust me. But I couldn't stop there; we were gilding the lily, after all. I found these mirrored frames on a discount rack at a department store; they're knockoffs of Venetian glass and add even more glimmer.

Layer upon layer of texture and color were added to the already ornate ceiling of this room. Six colors alone from top to bottom. Bold acrylic paint mimics the look of authentic gold leaf on the detailed moldings.

the details

A bouquet of fresh long-stemmed roses sets a romantic mood. Silk flowers aren't nearly as convincing, so stick with the Real McCoy when decorating with flowers. Wine-glasses make for creative candleholders. Soak the glasses in warm water and the burned wax will pop right out after use.

Finding a home for all of your belongings in a studio can be a real task. I hung a row of hooks down an entire wall for easy access to coats, towels, and robes.

The table and chairs are actually an outdoor dinette set I purchased at the end of the season for a remarkable discount ($75 for the entire set). The drapery treatments are in fact shower-curtain liners ($4 each). Their semitranslucent composition allows the light to glow around them, and their plastic texture mimics that of a fine taffeta (well, almost).

NEW USES: **POT RACKS**

Melanie's bed needed a headboard to define it as the focal point in this room. The royal bedrooms of Versailles were my inspiration: long, luxurious fabric draping from the ceiling. Unfortunately, I'm not on a French royal's budget, so I needed a cheap and easy solution to get the same look. While wandering the aisles of the kitchen department in my local superstore, I noticed the way the pots hung from a semicircular pot rack and thought, Voilà! My headboard. Bedsheets in a striking red were hung in lieu of fine silks and brocades. A shimmery mosaic mirror and flanking sconces finish off the regal look for much less than a king's ransom. (See how the headboard was constructed on page 34.)

the projects

POT RACK HEADBOARD

To create the look of a lavish French bed canopy, I didn't have to go any farther than the kitchen department at my local superstore. The pot rack and all the accessories cost less than $100, including the flanking sconces and mosaic mirror.

Items you will need:

Semicircular wall-mount pot rack

Screws

Screwdriver

Large S hooks (these are usually supplied with the pot racks, to hold the pots)

Drapery clips (can be found in most drapery departments of home stores)

Fabric panels—I used bed sheets, but you can use drapery panels or any hemmed fabric

Here's how you do it:

1. Affix the pot rack to the wall. Find a stud or use drywall screws for added security.

2. Next, hang the S hooks and the drapery clips from the pot rack.

3. Attach the fabric to the drapery clips.

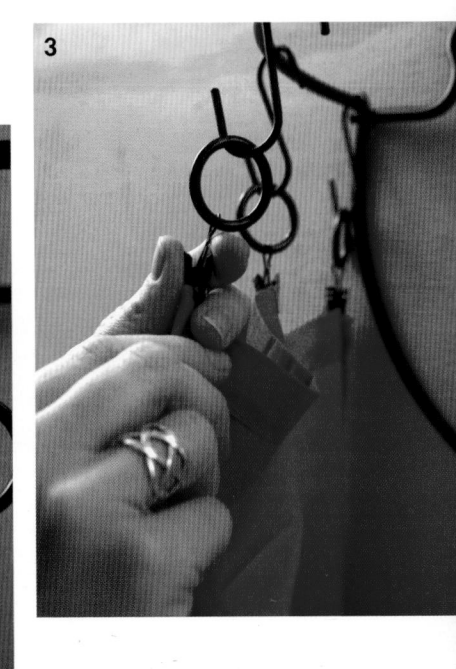

STARRY CEILING

I wanted to mimic the look of the nighttime sky in our studio. Although I didn't relish the thought of painting Melanie's ceiling (what a chore!), I knew I'd have to take on the task to complete the fantasy. This is actually a simple project; the only difficult part is the angle—your arms may start to cramp a bit. But the results are awesome. Remember to cover your floor with a tarp to avoid drips.

Items you will need:

Drop cloths

2 shades of dark blue paint—1 a shade lighter than the other (I used Connecticut Yankee for the base and Diplomat Blue for the rag roll coat)

1 gallon clear latex glaze

Paint rollers, brushes, paint trays

Terry-cloth rag

Several small bottles of acrylic paint (I chose a pearly gold tone, which can be purchased at any craft store)

Star stamps in several sizes (also available at any craft store)

Here's how you do it:

1. Cover the floor and the furniture with the drop cloths.

2. Paint your ceiling the darker of the two blues and allow it to dry. Mix the lighter blue with the latex glaze—one part glaze to one part paint. Dab a corner of the rag into the paint/glaze mixture, and rub it on the ceiling in a circular, irregular pattern. This step gives your ceiling texture and a cloudy, realistic look.

3. Press the star stamp into a small amount of acrylic paint. Make sure you have a nice, even coating on the stamp. Use different sizes in an irregular pattern for the most realistic look; use the same stamp size in a uniform pattern for a more formal alfresco look.

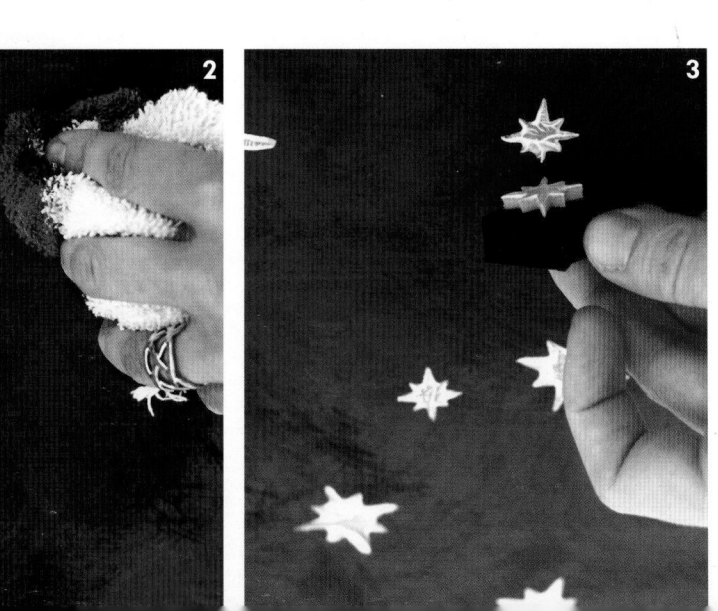

feminine dining room

IF YOU HAD TO SHOVE A MOUNTAIN OF PAPERS OVER TO SIT DOWN AND read this chapter, then *read on*, *baby*—this one's for you! Most of us have more things than we really need, and I'm sure a lot of us can identify with quickly cramming those extra items in a closet or a drawer when company comes a callin'. The difference between most of us and the pack rats of the world is that we periodically weed out the clutter, while the pack rats just keep on accumulating.

The first step to recovery is recognition. Look around your home: Do you have out-dated calendars, clothes that haven't fit since college, owner's manuals for appliances you don't own anymore? Then *you*, my friend, are a pack rat.

But there is hope. Here are a few tips to avoid being buried alive by all your junk:

- TAKE THE QUIZ. Ask yourself why you're keeping all this stuff. Is it for senti-mental reasons? If so, take photographs of the items, catalog the photographs, and trash the bulky stuff.

- RAID THE CLOSET. If you haven't worn it in two years, take it to Goodwill. Treat yourself to something new when you actually *do* lose those ten pounds.

- ACCEPT THE TRUTH. Okay, this will be the hardest one for you to take: Your Beanie Baby collection is not really valuable. Unless you're collecting gold bouillon, hardly any collection is worth as much as you think—lose it unless you love it.

- THROW A FAREWELL PARTY FOR ALL OF YOUR CLUTTER. Having your friends shame you into throwing away your garbage is great motivation.

the dilemma

Let me begin by saying that our homeowner Lena is a dear personal friend. She is by far the most stylish woman I've ever known— charming, intelligent, and incredibly talented at her profession. With that said, I am now going to publicly "out" her as a pack rat. In her defense, her case is mild. Her home is spotless, and the items she can't cut loose are arranged in tidy stacks. Her dilemma is common: Like millions of people in this country, she has developed sentimental attachments to her material possessions, and over time the possessions have begun to take over. She can't let go and needs help deciding which items to keep and which to throw away. It's going to be my mission to convince Lena she doesn't need these things anymore. She's ready for a change, and ridding herself of the clutter of the past will be the first major step. A total girlie-girl, Lena needs to flash some of her sparkling personality into this room. She will be hosting a family gathering in two weeks, so we have no time to lose.

AFTER

BEFORE

THE GOOD NEWS

- Lena has already bought a box of trash bags and is willing to use them.
- The table and chairs are nice and in good shape.
- Lots of natural light fills the room.
- The carpet is new and in good condition.

THE BAD NEWS

- We have years of belongings to sift through before we see the light.
- There are major privacy issues because the windows look out onto a public street.
- The large 1960s sheet mirror over the fireplace is broken and dated.

THE PLAN

I need to assist Lena in deciding which of her treasured items to keep, and then help her remove the rest. Once the room is cleared, bright dynamic colors will be brought in to suit her vibrant personality. New window treatments that admit light but preserve Lena's privacy will be needed. I will also make better use of the fireplace area. I've got two weeks and $500 to turn a storage facility into a feminine, vivid, and entertaining space.

THE GRAND TOTAL: $496.42

the color palette

One afternoon while shopping together Lena showed me a shower curtain she liked. She couldn't use it for her own bathroom because she has shower doors. While she contemplated removing the doors, I suggested we use the shower curtains as drapery treatments in her dining room. We bought three, and from that moment we had our plan. I simply pulled the lime green and salmon tones from the stripes in the curtains. Finding fabrics you love and working a color scheme around them is the easiest and most foolproof way to decorate a room.

PAINT COLORS

Walls: Frog Prince, Kelly-Moore KM3326-2

Hutch inset: Patient Pink, Kelly-Moore KM3661-2

Trim: Swiss Coffee, Kelly-Moore Standard

STORAGE

The key to a long-lasting cure for the pack rat is to provide precise locations to store items. For the office, a filing system is a must. And a recipe box in the kitchen will save you from rummaging through overstuffed drawers on Thanksgiving in search of your great-aunt's recipe for sweet potato pie.

In Lena's dining room I decided to bring in small baskets for her little odds and ends. Baskets are a wonderful way to store small items such as keys, pens, mail, and other objects that need to be readily available. Small baskets like these (IKEA, $5 each) are great because you can't see the clutter, plus they can contain only so much junk. Once they start to overflow, it's time to start throwing stuff out.

NEW USES: **PAPER**

Wrapping paper isn't just for the holidays. I used quite a bit of it in this room to tie the look together. We re-covered lamp shades and place mats—even framed the place mats as artwork. But don't stop at wrapping paper. Most art stores now have an abundant selection of specialty papers to fit any taste. I've used Japanese and French newspaper print with equally agreeable results. Check the yellow pages or the Internet for paper suppliers in your area.

the details

My inspiration for this room was the shower curtains we are now using for draperies. The transparent stripe of plastic material solves the challenge of a window treatment that would both allow in light and provide privacy.

I brought in coordinating dinnerware in bright colors to finish the look. We customized the place mats to match the artwork and lamp shades. (Check out page 43 to see how we pulled it off.)

We tore down the original behemoth of a mirror and replaced it with a smaller mirror with a silver-leaf trim. The scale of the new mirror suits the space to a T. Flanking the mirror are sconces for added mood lighting; we custom-covered the lamp shades with wrapping paper. (To see how it was done, go to page 42). Tea roses were added for a feminine touch.

Lena is a voracious reader, so I thought a seating area near the fireplace would be a nice spot for her to curl up with a good book; a fleece throw makes it even cozier. We painted the unfinished wicker chair and ottoman a muted bronze tone to coordinate with the existing dining furniture.

During the summer months, brighten up your fireplace with some greenery; these peace lilies are easy to care for and don't require lots of light.

the projects

LAMP SHADES

Custom lamp shades for chandeliers and sconces can really make the look in a room. But achieving this look can run you into the poorhouse—each shade will cost at least $40 in specialty home stores. Multiply that by two for sconces or five for chandeliers, and you can see what I mean.

I've found a surprisingly easy way to make your own custom shades for much less. At any craft or fabric store you can purchase self-adhesive lamp shades, which come in all standard sizes ($4.50 for sconce size and up to $14.99 for standard lamp size), and you can adhere anything to their gummy surface. They are sold with a paper backing that can be used as a template for the fabric or paper covering of your choice. This project is cheap and easy, and the design is totally your own.

Items you will need:

Self-adhesive lamp shades with paper templates

Pencil

Scissors

Fabric or paper for covering

Hole punch

Crystal chandelier prisms (these can be found cheap on eBay)

Here's how you do it:

1. Using the paper template provided with the self-adhesive lamp shade, draw your pattern onto the paper with the pencil and cut it out with the scissors.

2. Apply the covering material to the lamp shade. Note: The adhesive is not very forgiving if you are using paper. Make sure all edges are lined up before you adhere the paper.

3. Punch holes around the bottom edge of the shade to hang the crystals.

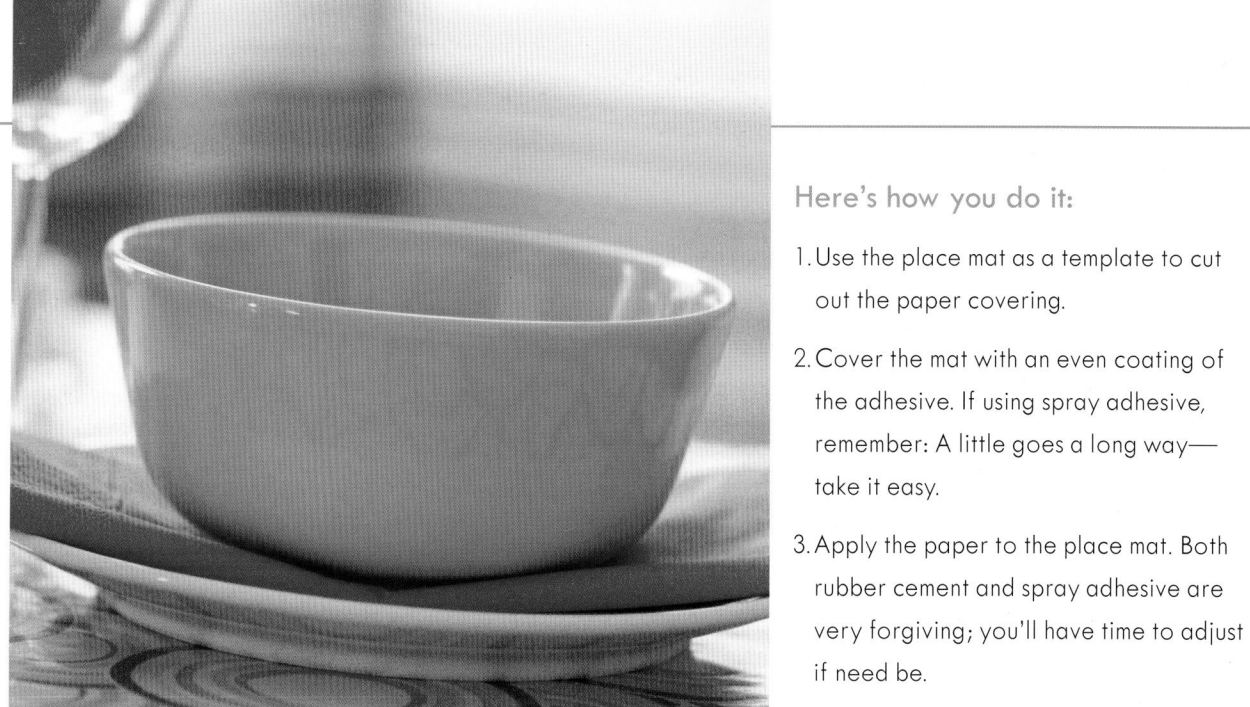

Here's how you do it:

1. Use the place mat as a template to cut out the paper covering.

2. Cover the mat with an even coating of the adhesive. If using spray adhesive, remember: A little goes a long way—take it easy.

3. Apply the paper to the place mat. Both rubber cement and spray adhesive are very forgiving; you'll have time to adjust if need be.

PLACE MATS

I wanted to add some pizzazz to Lena's dining table but couldn't find the right look. I decided to customize some inexpensive cork place mats with the same wrapping paper I used for our jazzy artwork and lamp shades. The great thing about this project is you can remove the paper after each event and change it easily.

Items you will need:

Cork, foam, or laminated place mats

Wrapping paper

Pencil

Scissors

Spray adhesive or rubber cement

gothic bedroom

MOST DECORATED ROOMS REVOLVE AROUND A THEME OF SOME SORT. THE theme may be subtle, like a consistent choice of style or color. But in some cases, the room is merely a vehicle for the theme. I remember a newspaper ad I once saw for a hotel in the Poconos. Each room was equipped with these gigantic martini-shaped hot tubs. Now *that's* a theme, I thought as I gazed upon the happy couple adrift in a sixteen-foot-tall cocktail. If your tastes run a bit obsessive, celebrate your unique sense of style. But also keep it in check with these bits of advice:

- KEEP IT REAL. Never buy anything from a gift shop at a theme park and use it for decoration in an adult home—ever. If you want to feel like a princess, do your research. Invest in period antiques (reproductions are fine) and lush fabrics.

- DON'T GO THEME CRAZY. Try to maintain a single theme throughout your home. Too many motifs in the same space can feel unsettling.

- DISPLAY COLLECTIONS TOGETHER. A majority of themes are based on a collection. If PEZ dispensers or smiley faces are your bag, display them all in one place for the most impact.

- ENJOY AND BE PROUD. Honey, if you've got the nerve and the ingenuity to transform your split-level ranch into an exact replica of Graceland, you've got my respect.

the dilemma

Our homeowner, Dracula (not his real name), has a certain look he likes for both himself and his home. Tattoos, black clothing, The Cure playing in the background . . . You know this guy. I realized I would be taking a walk on the dark side when he asked me to design a room around a rather ghoulish 7 by 5-foot oil painting of a tree with roots made of body parts. However, being a big fan of both Halloween *and* The Cure, I knew I could handle the job.

THE GOOD NEWS

- It will be easy to choose a color scheme. I will simply pull the tones from the inspirational artwork.
- The two baroque marble side tables will fit perfectly into the Gothic design I have planned.
- There aren't too many windows to let in the deadly light of day.
- A large sliding-door closet makes up an entire wall of the room, so storage is not an issue.
- A collection of antique gilt picture frames will work nicely into my design.

THE BAD NEWS

- There is no bed frame, just a mattress and box springs.
- The only lighting in the space is too modern for the old-world look we want. The lamps will have to be replaced.
- I'm scared. (Just kidding; The Count is really a cool guy.)

THE PLAN

I want to play up this Gothic theme by using deep, rich colors and period details. The large scale of the painting and the smaller size of everything else leave the room feeling unbalanced. I want to add height and scale to the bed in hopes of evening out this space. Electronics do not have old-world charm, so I plan to stow them in a small reading area off the bedroom. The overall mission will be to transform an ordinary bedroom into a lair fit for a vampire for less than $500.

THE GRAND TOTAL: $488.31

the
color
palette

The macabre oil painting might not be for everyone, but no one can deny its rich, dramatic tones. Choosing complementary hues for the room was an easy task: blood red for the walls, and accents as black as night. The sparkle of gold in our homeowner's side tables is carried throughout the space with a fleur-de-lis stamp and gold acrylic paint. This could easily be toned down for those who prefer a less ghoulish atmosphere, because the majority of the Gothic feel comes from the accessories. Consider the color palette alone, and it would work for many different styles.

PAINT COLORS

Walls: Terra Rosa,
Kelly-Moore AC19-R
Gold accents: Metallic Gold
(found at any craft store)

NEW USES: FRAMES

Frames are usually for displaying art. But in the case of our Gothic bedroom, a collection of antique frames *is* the art. This eye-catching arrangement couldn't have been easier to pull together. Once the walls were painted, I hung the frames along one wall. Using a rubber stamp and gold acrylic paint, I then stamped a fleur-de-lis motif in a formal pattern inside the frames' openings. This concept would work with any design—just change the type of frame and stamp: For a more modern space, sleek black frames with graphic geometric stamps can be used; shabby white frames with a floral stamp will add a touch of femininity to a young girl's room.

GONE TO THE DOGS . . .

There's another resident evil in this bedroom, and his name is Dante. He is a six-year-old Labrador retriever (black, of course), and I couldn't forget about him in my design. His doggy bed was in decent condition, but the cover was shabby. I seem to always have extra leopard-print fabric lying around (doesn't everybody?), so I tailored a removable slipcover. When decorating your own space, remember the details. A dog bed is a necessity if you have a dog. But if it's a hairy mess, your room will suffer for it. This newly re-covered dog bed gives the room a professional, finished appearance. If your pooch's bed has seen better days but you're not much of a seamstress, there are loads of specialty pet stores where you can find both custom dog beds and standard-sized covers in a variety of snazzy designs.

the details

A gargoyle stands watch over the sleeping area. (See how I transformed the plaster statuettes into lamps on page 50.)

The draping of old-world fabric at the head of the bed is fit for a vampire, so of course I had to include a mirror. (To learn how the draperies were hung, turn to page 51.)

This bolster pillow was re-covered by simply wrapping it in a cotton tapestry and tying the ends of the fabric in knots. This project will work equally well on standard or square pillows by tying the corners together diagonally.

Bloodred rose petals scattered across the stark white duvet bewitch the senses. These are made of silk so they can be reused. I found them in the bridal department of a craft store.

A faux crystal chandelier, purchased at a home consignment store for $24, illuminates a dark corner of the room.

the projects

GARGOYLE LAMPS

In my research for this room, I never got a straight answer on the exact history and purpose of the gargoyle in Gothic design. But I did find some amusing theories. One is the belief that their hideous appearance was used to ward off evil—the "Move along, Mr. Evil, we've got all the demonic stuff taken care of in here" philosophy. Another possibility is that they served as reminders of the perils of hell to parishioners—the "You don't want to end up like this" concept. There is even a myth that tells of how the gargoyles would come to life at night to protect the sleeping.

Regardless of their function, gargoyles have certainly served as a defining element in Gothic design, so this bedroom had to include a couple. The ones I found make frightful conversation pieces, but I also wanted them to serve double duty as light sources. I purchased these plaster statuettes from a fountain and statuary company for $37 each. If you were to wait until Halloween-time, I'm sure you could find fiberglass or plastic versions for much less.

Items you will need:

Gargoyle

Drill

Ceramic drill bit one size larger than the lamp rod

Protective eyewear

Lamp rod (can be found at any hardware store along with the lamp kit)

Lamp kit

Air-drying modeling clay the same color as your gargoyle

Here's how you do it:

1. First, drill a hole through the center of the gargoyle. If yours is plaster like mine, you will need a ceramic drill bit or the whole thing will likely explode, and there you'll be with gargoyle guts all over your head. Don't forget to wear the protective eyewear.

2. Next, run the lamp rod through the center of the gargoyle. Run the wiring from the lamp kit through the rod and connect the lamp according to the manufacturer's instructions.

3. Once you've finished, you may notice that the lamp rod is a bit wobbly. Press the air-drying clay into the recesses to secure the lamp.

DRAPERY HEADBOARD

The large scale of the homeowner's oil painting dwarfed the other furnishings, so I needed to add height to the bed to bring balance to the space. I decided to hang drapery panels from the ceiling. They not only correct the scale of the bed, but their triangular shape is also typical of Gothic design.

Items you will need:

2 ceiling hooks

Drill

Curtain rod

2 tab-top drapery panels

2 lengths of chain

2 large S hooks

Here's how you do it:

1. Insert the ceiling hooks over the bed according to the manufacturer's instructions.

2. Thread the curtain rod through the tabs of both drapery panels.

3. Hang the chains from the ceiling hooks. Attach the S hooks to the chains, and the rest of the curtain rod inside both S hooks.

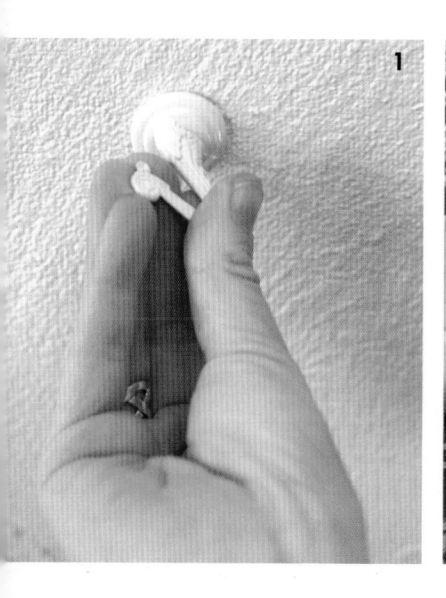

pop art bedroom

EXPRESS YOURSELF. YOUR BEDROOM SHOULD BE YOUR SANCTUARY, A RETREAT from the hectic pace of the everyday world. But that doesn't mean the room has to take itself so seriously. A retreat does not by definition have to include yoga mats and Enya music. If your idea of a sanctuary involves a disco ball and some beanbag chairs, knock yourself out! It's *your* retreat. Be a rebel and make it your own.

- LOOK AT YOUR WARDROBE. What colors are in your closet? Wild bright hues, or muted earth tones? Pull your interior colors from what you're comfortable wearing. Reserve the more trendy colors for inexpensive accessories, while keeping the big-ticket items more neutral for when the day comes that hot pink isn't in anymore.

- THINK YOU CAN'T AFFORD ART- WORK? Sure you can! Almost anything can be framed and hung on a wall— movie posters, decorative paper, fabric —just make sure the framing looks professional. In this chapter, we even made our own art. (See page 58 for details.)

- LIKE TO READ? Surround yourself with your favorites. Small bookcases make excellent nightstands for bookworms.

- BE YOURSELF. You will feel the most relaxed surrounded by the things you love, no matter what they are.

the dilemma

Melissa is an artist. Her funky two-bedroom apartment is filled with brightly colored collages, photographs, paintings, and even a dress form for all the stylish fashions she creates for herself and for her friends. So why is her bedroom so drab? When the decorating budget is meager, bedrooms can take a backseat to more public areas. Melissa has decided to tackle her plain bedroom with my help and would like to see a bright, fresh look for the lackluster space.

THE GOOD NEWS

- The bed and sheets are in good condition.
- The room gets lots of natural light.
- The hardwood floors are in excellent shape, so coverage can be simply cosmetic.

THE BAD NEWS

- The bed has no headboard.
- The duvet is shabby, not chic.
- The windows are an odd shape and at a weird level.
- There's not much existing furniture to work with.

AFTER

BEFORE

THE PLAN

I want to bring in bright, fun colors to liven up this boring white room. Next, I plan to create a headboard to make Melissa's bed more comfortable and more of a focal point. Artwork will be introduced for interest, and we'll add better lighting sources. A boring room will go from frumpy to fabulous for less than $500.

THE GRAND TOTAL: $463.64

the color palette

Melissa may have dared me by saying, "The brighter, the better." Her eccentric personality, artistic bent, and mod shag hairdo led me to base the room's color scheme around the pop art of Andy Warhol. His brilliantly hued silkscreen portraits of such celebrities as Marilyn Monroe, Elvis Presley, and Jackie O were first created in the 1960s but continue to make a lasting impression in the art world. Warhol's stylized use of bright, almost fluorescent, color and his rebellious attitude toward the highbrow establishment made him the perfect muse for this room.

Ruby red sheets were my first purchase. Their boldness draws the eye to the bed. I next chose an aquamarine hue for the walls. On the color wheel, blue tones are considered contrasting colors to red. High contrast adds drama and excitement, and that sense of activity was exactly what was needed to add spice to Melissa's drab bedroom. Black-and-white accents in the bedding, rug, and accessories add a crisp touch to the adventurous color scheme.

PAINT COLOR
Arizona Turquoise, Kelly-Moore KM319-2

WINDOWS

The windows in this room are an odd shape and size for the space. Their peculiar placement at the top of the wall makes you feel as if you are in a basement, and our homeowner felt claustrophobic and cramped in the space—and consequently avoided the room during waking hours. Creative window treatments would have to be made to remedy this situation. I installed floor-length drapery panels from a black curtain rod to fool the eye into thinking the windows are more proportionate to the room. Their length draws the eye downward and visually extends the window.

Think twice about the windows in your own home. There's a saying in interior design that goes something like "If you can't hide it, celebrate it." If disguising a defect in your home is just going to make it look worse, pretend you *meant* it to look that way in the first place. In our case, we could have taken another route. For instance, a large chest could have been placed under our odd-shaped window. Colored-glass pieces could have been situated on top of the chest to allow the natural sunlight to filter through, thus making the window a focal point instead of an eyesore.

the details

Keep your dirty laundry off the floor with these inexpensive containers. I got two: one for whites, one for colors.

Even a freaky room like this needs a touch of serenity. I found this fiberglass Buddha bird feeder on eBay for $24. A candle can be placed in the birdseed depository for an extra dose of chi. A small birdbath would also make a creative candleholder—just float the candles in the water. Visit your local nursery for inspiration.

NEW USES: **TRASH CANS**

Staying ahead of the laundry game is a worrisome task. And many of us don't have the luxury of a fully appointed laundry room to store all the dirty clothes awaiting the washer. Inevitably, soiled laundry ends up lying on the floor in places where it shouldn't. I wanted a depository for Melissa's laundry that would be inexpensive and easy to access, and would completely hide the clothes from view. What I *didn't* want was one of those rickety wicker numbers like your grandmother had. This is a hip room and it needs hip accessories. What I found were two low-cost plastic trash receptacles. They were cheap ($14 each), fit nicely under the console table, and are opaque so visitors don't have to see any unmentionables.

Think outside the hamper when looking for your own laundry bins. Container stores offer many choices that may not be intended for laundry per se but would work just as well. Hardware stores sell leaf bins and metal trash cans that would work for more industrial decors. Whatever you choose, stay away from those tacky wicker hampers—even if you *are* a grandma.

To paraphrase Andy Warhol, "Everyone will have her fifteen minutes of fame." So get step-by-step instructions for making your own funky self-portrait on page 58.

A leopard-print pillow adds texture to the simple red-and-white bed linens; a zebra print would work equally well. If animal prints aren't your thing, choose accents that contain colors from the room for a pulled-together look.

The most common focal point in a bedroom is, well, *the bed*. Unfortunately, Melissa's plain mattress and box springs were a tad "pointless." I created the look of an upholstered, tufted headboard for less than $50. (See how it was constructed on page 59.)

the projects

POP ART SELF-PORTRAIT

The artwork adds the right touch of Melissa's colorful personality to the room —and it was fun to create. The silkscreen portraits of Andy Warhol were the inspiration, but these masterpieces were much easier to produce.

Items you will need:

Photograph

Photocopier

Nonstreak markers in several bright colors

Scissors

Brightly colored art paper

Rubber cement

Picture frame with mat

Here's how you do it:

1. First, using the photocopier, enlarge the photograph on regular paper to fit the picture frame.

2. Next, color in the face as you like. Make up your own design or visit www.andy-warhol.org for inspiration.

3. Cut out the image using the scissors.

4. Place the image onto a sheet of the colored art paper for the boldest look. Use a dab of the rubber cement to secure the image in place.

5. Put the artwork into the frame.

PILLOW HEADBOARD

Every bed needs a headboard—not just for looks but also for comfort. Melissa is a book lover, and I can't imagine how unsatisfying it was to read on that bare mattress in the middle of the room. I wanted a cushy place for her to nestle up. What I found were three seat cushions and a curtain rod. The Velcro straps on the cushions make the project that much easier.

Items you will need:

Tape Measure

Pencil

Curtain rod brackets

Wall mounts and screws

Screwdriver

Drill

Curtain rod the width of your bed

3 or 4 seat cushions (depending on the size of your bed) with straps

Here's how you do it:

1. First, measure the height at which you want to hang the curtain rod. This is the most important step because if the rod is too low, your head will hit it when you sit in bed. The measurement will vary with every bed and every person.

2. Install the curtain rod brackets using the wall mounts and the screws. Place the curtain rod over the brackets just as if you were hanging window treatments.

3. Attach the seat cushions using the straps provided.

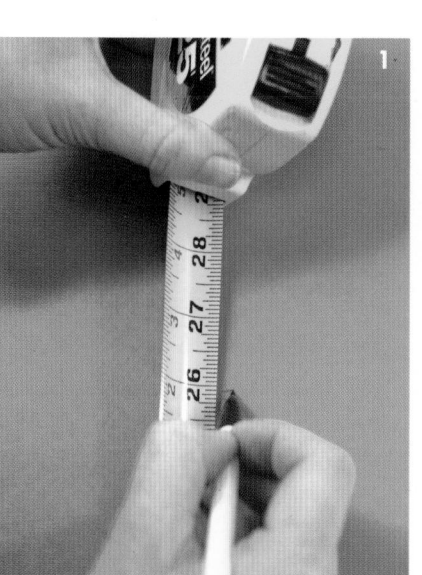

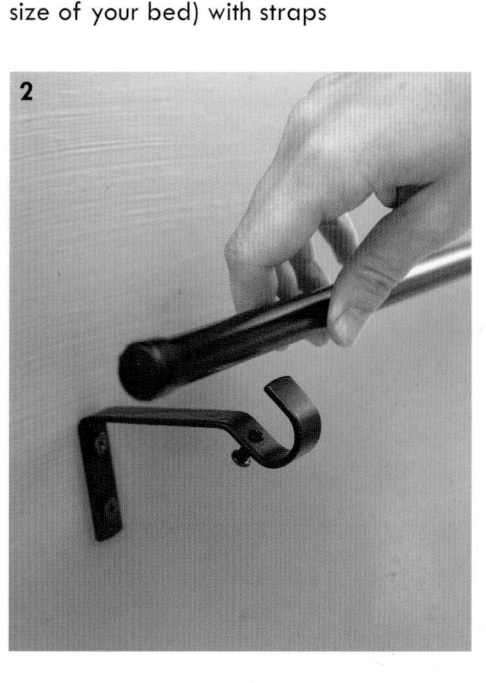

classic rooms

For the milder at heart, this section is dedicated to you. Traditional furnishings and organic color palettes define the styles of these spaces. Just because you may not fancy bold colors and busy patterns doesn't mean you have to reside in the House of Humdrum. There are many time-tested design choices and decorating tips to keep more classically themed rooms interesting:

- **AN ALL-BEIGE ROOM** can look mighty boring without any diversion. Keep monochromatic rooms from looking dull by introducing different textures. Nubby jute rugs, damask draperies, and chenille upholstery will add interest to your space.
- **MIX MODERN PIECES** with your more conventional items for a fresh, youthful look.
- **FLEA MARKETS,** consignment stores, and estate sales are fabulous resources for large, classic furnishings.
- **NOTHING IS MORE CLASSIC THAN NATURE.** Visit upscale gardening stores to get inspiration for timeless, organic style.

botanical dining room

DINING ROOMS CAN HAVE SO MANY USES: ENTERTAINING, EATING, DOING homework, laundry folding, even working from home. It's important to decide how you're going to use yours when making design decisions.

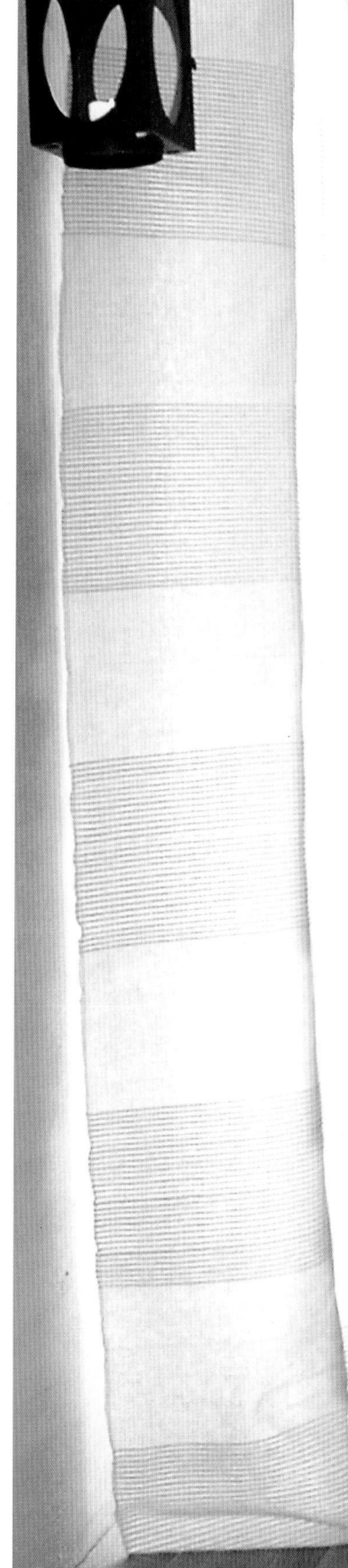

- **STORAGE IS THE KEY.** Storage is generally not a major issue for dining rooms. Buffets, hutches, or sideboards can usually handle the load of napkins, china, and silver. However, if your dining room is serving double duty as a home office or a storage area, chances are that books and boxes are taking over. Choose multipurpose furnishings that will adequately store your possessions while still making room for family dinners.

- **SET THE MOOD.** Most dining rooms have some sort of overhead light, but consider other forms of lighting. Table lamps placed on a buffet offer a nice alternative to the bright glare of an overhead fixture. Candlelight is always a nice option for those romantic dinners. But team candlelight with a dimmer switch on your overhead so you can see what you're eating.

- **MAKE ROOM FOR WORK.** If your home is square-footage-challenged, and your dining room needs to double as an office, consider computer hutches that hide all the paperwork—especially if your dining room opens out onto other public spaces. IKEA, Ethan Allen, and Pottery Barn offer nice, affordable choices (see "Resources," page 187).

the dilemma

Since the Harringtons moved into their 1950s ranch-style home three years ago, their dining room has been used for little more than a pathway to the kitchen. The children have outgrown the toys stored there, and the family is ready to transform this space into more of a dining/entertaining area. Mom has quite the green thumb—the gardens surrounding the property are meticulously groomed, and the house itself is filled with planting and landscaping literature. My goal is to bring this love of nature into their home.

THE GOOD NEWS

- Lots of natural light will enhance the organic mood I want.
- Although pretty scratched-up, the dining chairs are in decent shape. I may be able to use some of them.
- The homeowner has given me permission to raid her botanical books to use as artwork.
- This room is basically a blank canvas— the family is open to anything, and there are no existing items I have to accommodate.

THE BAD NEWS

- There is hardly any furniture.
- The dining table will have to be replaced because it's unsteady.
- There's no overhead lighting.

THE PLAN

I'd like to start by clearing the room of the unused toys, which the children have outgrown. I'm sure a charitable thrift store will be able to find new homes for all the

AFTER

BEFORE

forgotten playthings. Once the room is cleared, I plan to bring in warm colors and textures to the bland white walls. Mom's botanical prints will play a major role in accessorizing. And, finally, I'd like to create a message board where the family can communicate about doctor appointments and PTA meetings. The ultimate goal is to transform a cold, lonely walkthrough into a warm, inviting dining space for less than $500.

THE GRAND TOTAL: $489.35

the color palette

Vintage botanical prints from Mrs. Harrington's favorite book, *The Pressed Plant*, were my inspiration for the color scheme. Sage greens, burnt umbers, and warm golds abound in this historic collection of botanical specimens. My plan was to make the dining space appear to be a page pulled from this treasured text. The walls in the room were crying out for warmth and texture. We first coated them in a creamy, butter yellow latex paint. Next, we added layers of a mocha-hued glaze with a rag in a random, circular motion to give the room an aged patina—much like the antique prints that sparked the whole process.

PAINT COLORS

Base coat: Goldiluxe, Kelly-Moore KM3461-2
Latex glaze: Mocha, McCloskey (this premixed glaze can be found at most paint stores)

BRING THE GARDEN INDOORS

I wanted this room to appear as if we'd dragged everything in from the outdoors. With that in mind, I kept all the elements organic in nature: Rush mat, cotton fabrics, paper, fruit, vegetables, and live greenery give the room its gardenlike presence.

High-end gardening stores, popping up all over the country, are excellent resources for inspiration. Many of their items are too fabulous to just leave outside. Companies such as Smith & Hawken even carry home decor items along with their outdoor tools and accessories (see "Resources," page 187).

Another great source of outdoor decor is eBay (see "Resources," page 187). Type in "garden architectural" in the search field, and you'll find hundreds of items—worn columns, cast-iron planters, sculpture, fountains—most of which will look as good inside your home as out. Look in your yellow pages or on the Internet for architectural salvage yards. They are chock-full of indoor/outdoor treasures.

the details

Lanterns cast the warm glow of candlelight on diners from either side of the large sliding doors. They are hung on cast-iron shelving brackets, which can be found at any hardware or home store. These brackets come in many different styles to suit any taste, from traditional to contemporary.

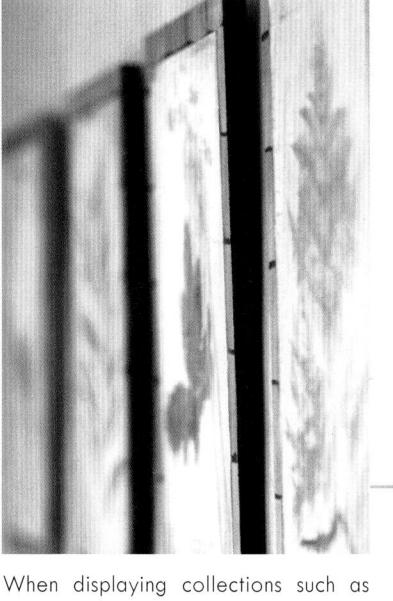

When displaying collections such as these botanical prints, keep a uniform thread among them to avoid a cluttered, disorganized look. These prints are all different but share the same framing. (To make this artwork yourself, check out page 69.)

I wanted light sources at different heights to add interest. The $500 budget didn't allow for proper sideboards to hold lamps, so inexpensive pine shelving does the job. An ample wicker trunk serves as storage for extra linens. Wicker lamp shades cast interesting shadows in the room, and their rustic texture adds to the organic mood.

Round wooden platters flank the new bulletin board. A message center is a must for the family on the go. (To see how I made this one, go to page 68.)

NEW USES:
GROCERIES

I always like to bring food elements into my designs for kitchens and dining rooms. On the sideboards I used dried beans to secure the candles in the glass bowls. Purchase the dried beans at the grocery store; they last for ages and can be easily replaced should they get waxy. Any dried legume would work; pick a color to match your own decor. I used the paper grocery bags to disguise the ugly plastic pots that came with our ferns. I simply rolled over the tops of the bags to form a lip, and then placed a small saucer and the plant inside. To ensure that your bags last longer, remove the plants when you water them.

A worn Indian rug, borrowed from the foyer floor, was cleaned and transformed into a casual and colorful table runner.

the projects

MESSAGE CENTER

When families are on the go, it's nice to have a place where you can leave notes and communicate with one another. I found an easy way to create an inexpensive message center for the Harringtons.

Items you will need:

Ready-made picture frame with mat (I found this one at IKEA for $20)

Chalkboard paint

Chalk

Here's how you do it:

1. First, remove the cardboard backing and the glass from the ready-made frame.

2. Next, apply the chalkboard paint to the cardboard backing.

3. Once the paint has dried, return the backing to the frame (without the glass) and leave a chalk-written message to someone you love.

BOTANICAL PRINTS

A love of nature was the inspiration for the room's design. I wanted to bring our home-owner's botanical print collection out from the bookshelf and onto the walls where she could enjoy it every day. The process used was decoupage, which you may remember from camp—we'd glue greeting cards onto blocks of wood for our parents. This process is exactly the same, except we've sub-stituted color copies for the greeting cards.

Items you will need:

Fiberboard cut to desired size (I had these cut to 10 × 13 inches)

Black spray paint

Botanical images (I made color copies from our homeowner's book because I didn't want to ruin the originals)

Decoupage glue

Sponge brushes

Black, sage green, and olive acrylic paint

Paint tray

Nonyellowing polyurethane

Picture-hanging kit

Hammer

Here's how you do it:

1. First, spray-paint the fiberboard black. Don't forget to paint the sides of the board as well.

2. Once the paint has dried, center the image on the fiberboard. Brush the glue underneath and over the top of the image. The paper may start to bubble; smooth out these bubbles gently with the sponge brush, starting from the middle and working your way out. Let dry.

3. For a more finished look, create a painted "frame" around your artwork. Loosely swirl the black, sage green, and olive acrylic paint in the paint tray. Dip the edge of the sponge brush into the mixture, and press the edge around the botanical image for a faux bamboo look. Once everything has dried, add a pro-tective coat of the nonyellowing polyurethane.

4. Using the picture-hanging kit and the hammer, attach the hanging hardware.

5. Hang your framed print on the wall.

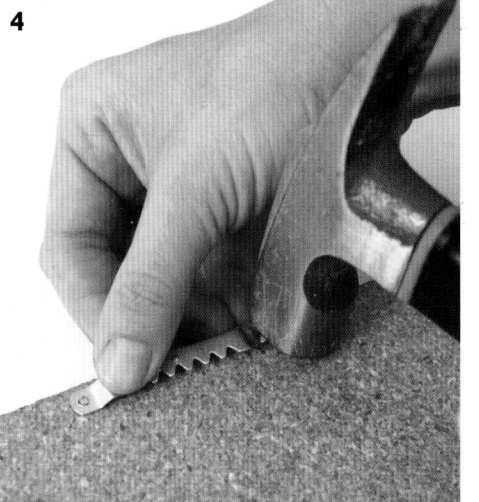

peaceful bedroom

PARENTS' RETREAT . . . PARENTING IS HARD WORK. AFTER PUTTING IN A FULL day at the office, grocery shopping, cooking, mopping up all the rejected food from the floor, checking homework, reading stories, brushing teeth, looking under the bed for monsters, and finally getting the kids to sleep, it's nice to have a place to go for some relaxation: A sanctuary where you can kick back, read, watch a movie, or just comb the peanut butter out of your hair. The bedroom can be a perfect haven for Mom and Dad at the end of the day. Consider your options when shopping for furnishings:

- **BITE THE BULLET.** In this book, I am forever showing you ways to shave money off your budget. But for some items you need to go ahead and shell out the money. Your mattress is one example. Do your homework and invest in a high-quality mattress that provides comfort and the right support. Expect to pay $700 to $1,000 for a good mattress. But it should last you eight to ten years.

- **MOVIE NIGHT.** Invest in a mini—entertainment center for your bedroom. A small television with a DVD player and a stereo will help you relax at the end of the day. Hide the clutter of electronics in a small hutch or armoire.

- **READING IS FUNDAMENTAL.** Dedicate a drawer in your nightstand to books, magazines, and journals. If you're a big reader, substitute short bookcases for night tables. Lamps can be placed on top, and you can have access to your library without leaving your bed.

the dilemma

The Santoses have two small children, and they designed their home with much thought for the needs of the family as a whole: comfortable and durable seating, play areas, and an impressive entertainment center fill the public areas. However, Mom and Dad would like to see a more peaceful, mature theme for their master bedroom—a parents' retreat from a sea of LEGOS and SpongeBob. They like the idea of a monochromatic color scheme and made attempts at a white-on-white minimalist look. Unfortunately, the results left them underwhelmed. They'd like to see some life brought into this room but without the use of any loud colors or patterns.

THE GOOD NEWS

- The room is large (17 by 15 feet).
- The mattress and box springs are in excellent condition.
- The cream-colored wall-to-wall carpet will work nicely with a neutral, monochromatic theme.

THE BAD NEWS

- The mirrored headboard is dated and old.
- The minuscule nightstands are not the right scale for the room and are greatly disproportionate to the massive California king bed.
- The drapery panels are too short for the wall.
- The current all-white color scheme is cold and has an institutional feel.

THE PLAN

A monochromatic color scheme of neutral earth tones will keep the peaceful mood, but texture and subtle patterns will make it interesting. I'll remove the old headboard

AFTER

BEFORE

and create one that's more timeless. Draping window treatments and new lighting will create ambience. I plan to turn this cold, white room into a cozy parents' retreat for less than $500.

THE GRAND TOTAL: $479.18

the color palette

The Santoses wanted a soothing, peaceful look for their master bedroom, so I chose a neutral, monochromatic scheme using different values of the same hue. For an example of a monochromatic scheme, look at a paint swatch strip, which has several different values of one color. Using two or more of the choices in a room creates a stylish and calming look. (White and black are generally considered neutral tones and can be added to the mix for interest.) For this room I chose golden tan for the walls, cocoa for the bed linens, and cream accents for a warm, soft feel.

FABRICS TO DYE FOR

We dyed the white cotton sheets in this room a warm cocoa brown to coordinate with the new headboard and bedding. This is an unpredictable and somewhat messy process, but it's an inexpensive way to refashion certain textiles in your home. Here are a few pointers on getting custom fabrics to dye for:

- Dyes usually work best on natural fabrics such as cotton, linen, and hemp. It's best to perform a swatch test to ensure that your fabric will absorb the dye evenly.

- The fabric should be washed to remove any dirt or sizing (a chemical used by dry cleaners and textile manufacturers to add body and luster to fabrics) that may interfere with the dye process. Don't dry; fabrics should be thoroughly wet for dyeing.

- Read the manufacturer's instructions as to how much dye you should use. To achieve the richest dark tones, ignore the instructions and double up on the dye.

- Always clean your washing machine after dying fabrics. The best way is to run a complete cycle with bleach and hot water.

FOR SMALLER PROJECTS: Fill a large bucket or container with enough warm water to completely cover the fabric. You want enough room for the fabric to be loosely stirred during the process. (Avoid using the bathtub or sink, however, as porcelain can stain.) Add the fabric, 2 cups salt, and $\frac{1}{4}$ cup dye fixer, which can be found at any craft or fabric store along with the dyes. The more the fabric is agitated, the more evenly the dye will affect the material. So stir till the cows come home, or until you achieve the desired depth of color. Rinse with cool water until the water runs clear, then wash in the washing machine.

FOR LARGER PROJECTS: If you have lots of fabric to be dyed the same color (as I had with these sheets), you can use the washing machine from the start. Once again, the fabric should be wet before starting. Fill the washing machine with warm water. Add the dye, about 5 cups salt, and $1\frac{1}{2}$ cups dye fixer. Agitate for 5 to 10 minutes. Once the dye has dissolved, submerge the wet fabric in the dye bath and agitate for 1 hour (or half that time for pastel shades). Allow the machine to run through the rinse cycle and spin.

PAINT COLOR
Gold Mountain, Kelly-Moore KM3452-2

the details

A simple, elegant way to add a touch of nature to any room is to fill a glass bowl with river rocks and a candle.

Back home, we would call the homeowners' curtains "high waters"—much too short for the wall. New, longer panels finish the look in this room. (See what these fabric panels really are, below.)

NEW USES:
BEDDING

Texture, pattern, and continuity are important elements in a monochromatic design. Without these components, a room can feel unfinished and boring. When searching for new bedding for the Santoses, I wanted simple color but significant pattern. I found a lovely cotton bedspread in a pale cream with subtle horizontal ribbing for interest. I bought a king size for the bed and four twin sizes to hang as window treatments. A bedspread may not be the first thing that pops into your head when you are thinking about draperies, but these work beautifully. The repeating color and texture add continuity to the room.

When coordinating your bedroom, take a long look in the bedding department. "Beds in a bag" are wonderful ways to pull together a look—and not just on the bed: Use the duvet on your bed and the sheets as curtains.

Without texture and pattern, a monochromatic room can look dull. Interest was added to the bed with a loosely woven wool throw and a new tufted headboard. (Learn how to make the headboard yourself on pages 76–77.)

Looped fringe was purchased at a fabric store and hot-glued to the edges of plain lamp shades. Dressmaker details such as upholstery trim and fringe give a room a professional finish.

The homeowners' tiny nightstands were dwarfed by their immense California king bed. The larger size of the new nightstands is more proportional to the bed and makes for better storage.

the projects

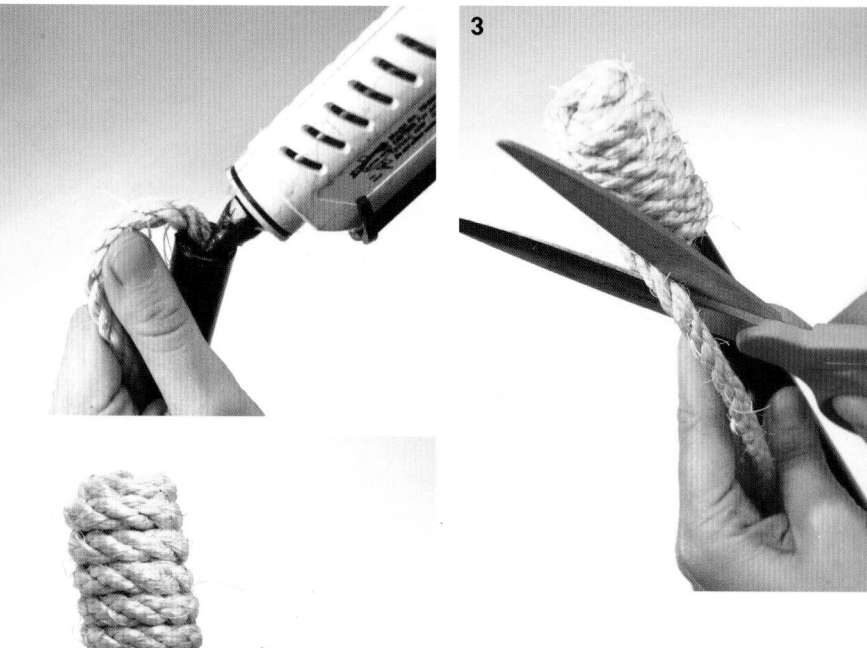

ROPE FINIALS

A good friend and fellow interior designer named Melissa Wilson showed me this clever trick to add a sophisticated detail to ordinary curtain rods using rope. Her technique involved a series of intricate sailor's knots, but she dumbed down a version for me using hot glue, and now I employ it frequently.

Items you will need:

Curtain rod

Rope

Hot-glue gun and glue sticks

Scissors

Here's how you do it:

1. First, remove the end cap of the curtain rod and place the end of the rope inside the opening; using the glue gun, secure with the hot glue.

2. Next, start wrapping the rope around the rod, securing with the hot glue as you go.

3. Once you've reached your desired length, cut the rope. Done!

1

2

3

TUFTED HEADBOARD

The Santoses' original mirrored headboard was hopelessly trapped in the eighties. They wanted a fresher, more contemporary look. I wanted to bring in a traditional headboard that would stand the test of time. As usual, my budget would not allow for any fancy store-bought bed frames, so I would have to make something myself. (I've probably made more than three hundred of these headboards in my career—they involve no sewing, and the results are amazing.)

Items you will need:

Plywood cut to size (the width should match your mattress, but the height can vary according to your own taste—this one was cut to 6 × 3 feet for a California king bed)

2-inch-thick upholstery foam, cut to the same size as the plywood

Quilter's batting: enough to cover the headboard with a 3-inch allowance on all sides

Fabric of your choice: enough to cover the headboard with a 3-inch allowance on all sides

Staple gun with ¼-inch-deep staples

Tape measure

Sharpie or marking pen

Scissors

1½-inch screws and washers

Screwdriver, preferably electric

Covered buttons (found in the notions department of any fabric store; they allow you to make custom buttons using your own fabric)

Hot-glue gun and glue sticks

Here's how you do it:

1. Layer your materials in this order: plywood, foam, batting, and fabric. The fabric and batting should have at least a 3-inch overhang on all four sides.

2. Flip the entire piece over, pull the fabric taut, and staple the fabric and batting around the entire plywood and foam base. Start with the sides and finish on the corners for the most professional look.

3. To begin the tufting process, decide where you'd like your buttons to go (a symmetrical grid pattern looks best—use the tape measure to ensure balance). With the Sharpie, make tiny marks where the buttons will go. Puncture small holes in the fabric with scissors. Using the screwdriver, insert and tightly affix the screws with the washers to the plywood back. The washers will keep the screws from slipping through the fabric. If the screws get caught in the batting and foam, simply use the scissors to cut a small "tunnel" through the batting to the wood.

4. Cover the buttons with the fabric. Using the glue gun, attach them with the hot glue onto the screw head and firmly press down until the glue dries.

5. To secure to the wall, I attached plywood strips to the back of the headboard, with small screws to serve as legs, and screwed the legs into the studs of the wall.

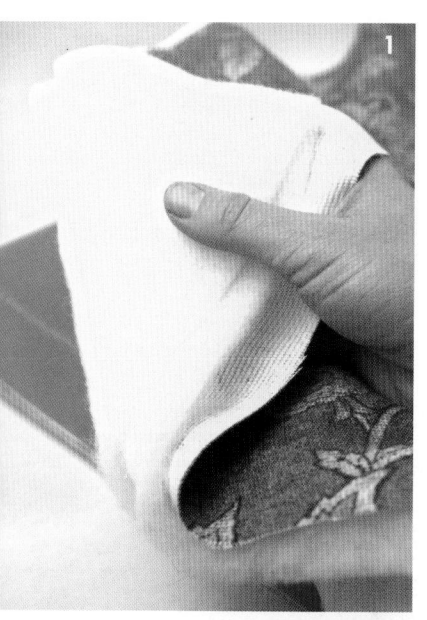

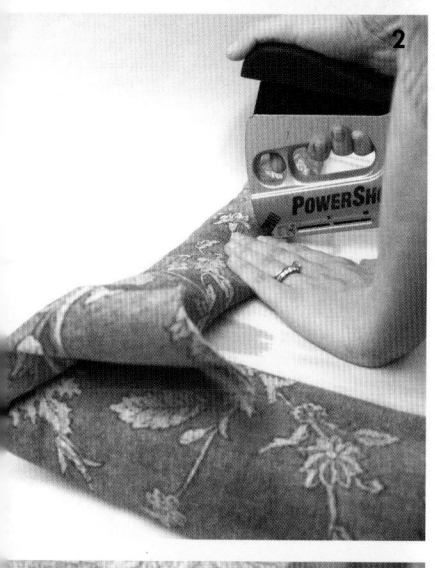

floral workspace

MANY OF US DON'T HAVE ENOUGH SPACE, SO ROOMS MUST SERVE DOUBLE duty: The home office/guest room combo is the most common. Much thought should go into the design of these areas so you can be productive and your guests can be comfortable. Here are some tips that should help:

- MAKE THE MOST OF WHAT YOU'VE GOT. Multipurpose rooms need multipurpose furnishings. Futons, daybeds, and convertible sofas will comfortably sleep your guests. Once they're gone, simply fold up the bed, and you have a cozy reading niche. Shop for storage cabinets that can double as temporary dressers for your guests. And if you like a clock in your office, make sure it has an alarm.

- STORAGE AND STYLE ARE KEY. If you're expecting guests, this is the perfect time to go through and throw out all the old paperwork and clutter in your office/guest room, and find permanent locations for everything you need to keep. Neither you nor your guests should have to keep moving boxes of books and papers around this room. It's also important to keep the room feeling homey. Don't let the office part take over and make the room feel institutional.

- R-E-S-P-E-C-T. This is your guests' room while they are visiting. Don't barge in to do business without running it past them first. Consider moving any current business to a temporary, makeshift location while your visitors are in town.

the dilemma

Noreen is ready to make a change in her cold, dismal office space. She has tried out a few shades of turquoise wall paint but hasn't been happy with any of her choices. So busy at work and so frustrated with her own decorating attempts, she'd just like to see the room done. And that's where I come in. The hodgepodge of storage options is inadequate, and the pale mauve walls are not her style. She's in here all day, every day, and would like a cozy, feminine workspace that could also accommodate sleepover guests.

THE GOOD NEWS

- A recently purchased wood and frosted-glass desk set will work nicely with my design.
- The neutral, laminate flooring is in good shape.
- The room has a spacious, symmetrical layout.

THE BAD NEWS

- The rickety bookshelves are overstuffed and add to the cluttered feel.
- The window treatments are terrible, twisted, and dusty.
- The bare floors make the room seem cold.

THE PLAN

Noreen needs to go through all the books and papers filling this space and throw out anything she doesn't need. I want to streamline this office and eliminate unnecessary clutter. New, more stylish storage will be introduced and soft, feminine colors will grace the entire room—all for less than $500.

THE GRAND TOTAL: $488.43

AFTER

BEFORE

NEW USES: **SHOWER-CURTAIN LINERS**

I'd like to take this opportunity to implore all of you who own vertical blinds to remove and destroy them. They are just awful and will never be a fashionable choice for any room—not even a dentist's office. Trust me, you'll feel better once they're gone.

Removing these eyesores was my first task in Noreen's office. But I needed to find a cheap alternative for window treatments, as I'd spent most of my budget on the futon and area rug. To give the office a fresh, more contemporary look, I replaced the heinous vertical blinds with sleek, stainless-steel *horizontal* blinds found at a discount home store ($20). To soften the edges, I hung shower-curtain liners. Their semitranslucent texture allows soft light to enter the room, their pale blue color coordinates perfectly with the color scheme, and at $3 each the price could not be beat. Liners come in many colors these days; I even think the clear ones would be groovy in the right room.

the color palette

To get the soft, feminine look for her home office/guest room, I pulled the colors for the space from a wool area rug I found at a consignment store. The rug's muted shades of pale gold and smoky powder blue were just what I'd envisioned. I literally held my paint swatches against the rug to get the best match. When trying to achieve a peaceful, soft look, choose colors that have the same value or intensity. High contrast adds drama and vivacity, while low contrast is easier on the eye and exudes calm.

PAINT COLORS

Walls: Sea Oats, Kelly-Moore KM3484
Accent wall: Barefoot Beach, Kelly-Moore KM3982-3
Bulletin board: Acapulco Aqua, Kelly-Moore KM3221-2

ON CONSIGNMENT

I love consignment-store shopping: You can get fantastic deals on furnishings for any area of your home. When I started shopping for this room's area rug, I had major trouble finding anything decent within my price range. You get what you pay for with new rugs; the cheaper ones are, well, *cheap*. I wanted a high-quality rug, but I didn't want to pay retail. After two weeks of hitting all my favorite consignment shops, I finally found this gorgeous 100-percent-wool rug for $85. I will admit it was a bit dirty and worn when I found it. But after a good scrubbing, it is not only an outstanding feature in this room, but it was the inspiration for the whole color scheme as well.

I got lucky finding this rug. The inventory in a consignment store changes frequently, and you never know what you'll find. The most useful advice I can give is to go early and often to get the best deals. And ask employees on which day of the week their new arrivals are delivered, to get a head start on the bargains.

the details

Decorative accents make this practical futon more fashionable. The small powder blue pillow was given a touch of class with the addition of a silk gerbera (a dab of hot glue secures the bloom in place). Geometric patterns add interest to the back wall. We made this artwork ourselves by using some leftover paint. (Learn how on page 85.)

A quick sanding and a new coat of paint gave Noreen's old chest of drawers a face-lift. The faux drawer pulls were created by masking off small rectangular areas on each drawer using painter's tape. I used the same blue paint we used on the bulletin board. The retro aluminum chairs were part of a discounted outdoor set I got for a steal ($9 each), and can be used as extra seating or as a landing for guests' luggage.

Do we really need all these books? I convinced Noreen to get down to the bare bones of her collection, which was taking up too much space. Once we whittled down her impressive accumulation, it was time to update the storage with sleek, floating shelves. Unless you have a proper library, an excess of literature can get in the way of daily life.

Noreen's office needed organization. We gave her a funky but feminine bulletin board using a new line of magnetic paint and silk gerbera daisies. (Do it yourself on page 84.)

This workspace can now double as a guest room. A futon is a practical choice for multipurpose rooms.

the projects

BULLETIN BOARD

Every office needs a bulletin board on which to place papers and little reminders. We made Noreen's out of a fairly new product called Magic Wall Magnetic Paint, which allows magnets to stick to your wall. It has a dull, silvery appearance, but once it's dried, you can paint any color over the top. It took us five coats before we could get anything to stick, but after that it worked like a charm.

Items you will need:

Level or chalk line to make straight lines

Pencil

Painter's tape

1 quart Magic Wall Magnetic Paint

Paint roller and tray

Regular latex paint in the color of your choice

Magnets

Silk gerbera daisies

Glue

Here's how you do it:

1. Using the level, pencil, and painter's tape, mask off the area for the board.

2. Next, apply at least four coats of the magnetic paint, allowing each coat to dry in between applications.

3. Paint the color of your choice over the magnetic paint and allow to dry.

4. Make the floral magnets by simply gluing the silk gerbera daisies to ordinary magnets.

WALL ART

For those who don't want to think too much about the art in their homes, this is the perfect project. I made these paintings using leftover paint from the room for a perfect match. The geometric shapes are easy to paint and are in keeping with the simple lines of the room. For the circle, I traced around a paint can with a pencil, then painted around the lines. For the slightly more complicated striped paintings, I used painter's tape.

Items you will need:

Prestretched canvases

3 different colors of paint

Paintbrushes and/or mini rollers

Measuring tape

Painter's tape

Here's how you do it:

1. First, paint each canvas a different color. Once they've dried, use the measuring tape to divide each canvas into three equal sections, and then mask them off with the painter's tape.

2. Paint the side sections different colors, leaving the center section alone.

3. Remove the tape, let dry, and you have instant art.

jade living room

COLOR IS AN INTEGRAL PART OF ANY INTERIOR DESIGN PROJECT. WHEN USED correctly, color can create balance, mood, and cohesion. Paint is usually the least expensive and easiest way to make an impact on a room. But those of you who have gasped in horror at the newly painted room that looks *nothing* like the tiny chip you picked out at the hardware store will agree: This task of bringing the right mix of colors into your home can be a risky business. We live in a world with an abundance of color choices, but with so many to choose from, finding the perfect palette can seem overwhelming. Patience and some practical tips will help you along the way:

- READ A BOOK. Scores of interior-design and decorating books specialize in color palettes and color theory. Many (like this one) will offer specific paint colors to make the search even easier. If you find a shade in a book you like but can't find the brand or name, simply take the swatch to a paint company specializing in color matching. Technology now allows for almost any hue to be duplicated.

- BE PROFESSIONAL. Seeing the whole package together makes it much easier to visualize the finished project, so interior designers create sample boards to display their ideas for color schemes and fabric choices. Try this yourself: Collect swatches or photographs of your current furnishings, and pair them with the paint chips and fabric samples you would like to use. This board can be as simple as a few paint chips and fabric swatches stapled to a piece of paper, and it will be a useful reference tool to take shopping.

- AVOID COMMITMENT. To spare yourself the anguish of painting an entire room the wrong color, use a decorator trick: Purchase sheets of white poster board at the craft store. Select several shades of paint and buy quarts (some manufacturers now offer inexpensive sample bottles of their most popular colors that cover about two square feet). Paint the poster boards and tape them to your walls, changing the location various times over the course of a few days. This will give you a clear idea of how light affects the tone throughout the day and will give you more confidence when you finally decide to commit.

the dilemma

Jennifer has recently purchased her first home. After finding places for all her belongings, she is unsatisfied with the home's general lack of style. Although she's made some efforts, Jennifer's biggest challenge has been creating a pulled-together look. She'd like to tackle the more public spaces first, and the living room is where she wants to start. Jennifer would like to see a refined, contemporary look for her living room.

THE GOOD NEWS

- The room is large (14 by 20 feet).
- The flooring is in good shape.
- The drapery panels are new, and we all like them.
- The sofa is in fair condition, and its neutral color will work well with any design.

THE BAD NEWS

- The room has an odd layout with ill-defined spaces.
- Most of the furnishings are old and mismatched, adding to the unbalanced feel.
- The walls are too stark.

THE PLAN

Jennifer's biggest problems in this room are proportion and color. I plan to pull this room together by eliminating unnecessary furnishings and bringing in pieces that will work together in scale and color. I will create a fresh, youthful look with more contemporary furnishings, and then illuminate the space with bursts of light—all for less than $500.

THE GRAND TOTAL: $498.92

AFTER

BEFORE

the color palette

Jennifer loves green. She introduced the hue into her living room with an olive futon cover and a hunter green area rug; jade and rubber plants line a corner bookcase. The problem is that the two shades of green clash somewhat, and their placement (two green items in a sea of white) makes for an unbalanced feel. Colors should coordinate and be repeated throughout a space to achieve harmony. I chose to paint all the walls in her favorite color of jade—this blanket of color gives the room cohesion and a more structured appearance. The furnishings are left neutral, and accents in ebony, chartreuse, and animal prints are a modern twist on traditional British colonial design.

PAINTING LIKE A PRO

I paint almost every room I make over for instant dramatic impact. The vibrant jade walls certainly made the most significant difference in this room, but color is only one aspect of starting a paint project. We're adults now; the days of slapping a flimsy, single coat of a cheap watery paint onto our walls are over. Beauty is in the details, and with these few tips you can get a professional finish in your own home:

• *Opt for quality.* Paint is cheap. Even the top brands should not cost you more than $50 for an average-sized room, $100 for a larger room with trim. But the *super*-cheap paints tend to be watery and don't cover as well. Invest in high-quality paints to save time and money in the long run. Next, decide which finish will be the best for your particular room. Flat or matte finishes hide imperfections but are more difficult to clean. Glossy finishes reflect light and are easiest to clean but will amplify every blemish on your wall. Satin finishes are the best compromise. And don't stop at high-quality paints: Invest in good brushes as well. My favorite brand is Purdy (see "Resources," page 187). They cost more but are worth it.

• *Preparation is everything.* Lay out a tarp. No matter how careful you think you are, Murphy's Law states that "Anyone Not Using a Tarp Must Drip Paint on the Most Valuable Upholstered Furnishing in the Room" (or something to that effect). Spackle all cracks and nail holes (seriously, the paint *will not* fill these holes). Caulk wood casings and cracks in the baseboards and moldings. Seal any stains or watermarks with a stain sealer (purchased at paint stores), then hand-sand any lumps and bumps your spackle may have left. Tape off anything that will not be painted, such as trim, electrical outlets, and light fixtures.

• *Paint like a pro.* Begin by "cutting in" with a brush around trim and corners. Fill in with a roller. Almost all paint colors will need a second coat. Darker shades and red hues may need more. If you are unsure about another coat, allow the paint to dry and look for spots missed.

• *Be a mean cleaning machine.* There is nothing more tedious than rinsing a loaded paintbrush—it seems as if the paint will never quit coming out. Many of us do a shoddy job out of sheer hopelessness. But leaving any amount of paint in a brush will ruin it. The same goes for rollers and trays; paint left in a tray can mix with the next color you use and spoil your effort. If you've made the investment in good tools, take the time to clean them properly. Decorator tip #420: Use liquid fabric softener to help loosen wet paint from brushes and rollers.

PAINT COLOR
Green Jeans, Kelly-Moore KM3335-3

the details

Colorful throw pillows can make a boring sofa more charismatic. I chose lush fabrics in chartreuse, rich browns, and zebra stripes to coordinate with the other accessories.

The overhead light source that casts warm candlelight over Jennifer's new seating area is an unusual choice for a living room. (See what its original purpose was on page 92.)

Bottled water for $7.50?!?! Set up your own mini-bar without the minibar price. I placed a few martini glasses, an ice bucket, and a shaker on one of the side tables for impromptu parties.

An inexpensive rush floor mat was hung on the wall to add scale and importance to our homeowner's existing artwork. Think of alternative wall hangings in your own home: Floor coverings, tapestries, and decorative blankets can all make appealing wall art.

Bamboo gardening stakes make a bold statement as an organic centerpiece on Jennifer's new coffee table. I cut the four-foot stalks to a more manageable size using a circular saw, then placed them in a glass vase. Nurseries and gardening stores are great resources for unusual home accessories.

NEW USES: **POT RACKS**

Lighting is one of the most effective ways to build depth and create mood in a room. Light sources from different angles and in varying intensities can add interest to any space. My first lighting choices for Jennifer's living room were silver wall sconces with black lamp shades to filter the light into appealing conical patterns on the wall. I wanted to add another layer of light cascading from above, but there was no electricity running to this area of the ceiling. My plan was to find a hanging fixture to provide overhead candlelight. I was disappointed to find that all of the chandelier-type candleholders in my budget were too small and dainty for this project. I needed a creative alternative.

I found exactly what I was looking for with the pots and pans. This rectangular ceiling-mounted pot rack has the clean, modern shape and substantial scale needed for this room. Plexiglas was cut to size and used to secure a collection of large pillar candles on the rack's surface. This transparent base allows even more light to be cast below and can be easily removed for cleaning. The repurposed pot rack was hung from the ceiling using ceiling hooks, just as it would be hung in a kitchen.

the project

CHALKBOARD ART

You've heard of mood rings? Well, this project is mood art. The medium is chalkboard paint and chalk, so as your mood changes, so can your decor: Simply wipe it off and start over. Not being much of a fine artist myself, I chose curlicues for my design. You can create geometric patterns, random words or quotes, or something more ornate. This project is super-easy and a lot of fun.

Items you will need:

Chalkboard spray paint

Prestretched canvas

Bamboo gardening stakes (found at any nursery or gardening store)

Miter or circular saw

Hot-glue gun and glue sticks

Chalk

Picture-hanging kit

Hammer

Here's how you do it:

1. First, apply the chalkboard paint to the canvas. Several light coats are better than one globby coat.

2. Next, cut the bamboo stakes to size with the saw, and then hot-glue them to the borders of the canvas.

3. The last step is to draw your design and hang it, using the picture-hanging kit and the hammer. (I simply hung the back of the canvas from a screw in the wall, but you could get fancy and buy the hanging hardware.)

1

2

3

luxe patio

AN EXTERIOR SPACE WHERE YOU CAN SIT AND COMMUNE WITH NATURE CAN ease the senses and relax the soul. It can also extend the usable square footage of your home and introduce additional entertaining areas by creating an outdoor room. Many homes have a designated patio or deck space, but you could also take over a porch, a small balcony, or a corner of the yard. Size is not as important as how you use the space.

- CONSTRUCT WALLS, SEATING AREAS, AND A FLOOR. To give your outdoor retreat the cozy feel of a real room, you will want to place objects in a certain way to suggest the feeling of containment. Plant bamboo stalks or place large potted plants along the boundaries of the space, which will add privacy and color. Decide how you will be using the area, and choose comfortable furnishings that will best suit you and your guests. Place straw mats on the ground to define the areas, or even paint a faux rug on the cement or wood flooring.

- SET THE MOOD. Outdoor speakers, a fire pit or chiminea (small clay fireplaces), propane patio heaters, landscaping, and mood lighting such as tiki torches and lanterns will add charm and interest. Visit restaurants and hotels with outdoor seating to get inspired.

- USE THE ROOM. During the warmer, drier months, make time each day to spend in your new refuge. Read, eat, entertain, or just relax and enjoy nature in your soothing getaway.

the dilemma

This patio is not being used for anything more than storage. The adjoining back stairs lead to a parking area, so this dismal landing is the first thing you see as you enter the home. Needless to say, the home-owners would like a more welcoming appearance. They'd love to entertain out here (the view is lovely), but with the lack of seating and the grungy surroundings they tend to steer their guests indoors. A spa look, complete with teak furnishings and crisp white fabrics, is what these folks would like to see for their deck: soft, cool, and peaceful.

THE GOOD NEWS

- The abundance of trees and greenery surrounding the deck will add to the spa-inspired design.
- There is electricity running out here, so I can add mood lighting.
- The space is large (10 by 17 feet).

THE BAD NEWS

- There is no furniture to speak of.
- The floor is a grimy plywood.
- The bare-bulb overhead lighting is depressing.
- There is no privacy from the parking area below.

THE PLAN

First impressions mean a lot, and this patio is making a bad one. I plan to give this space a spa-like ambience. Rich wood tones, stone, fire, and water will awaken the senses, while peaceful sounds will ease the mind. I will bring in comfortable seating and proper lighting, all for less than $500.

THE GRAND TOTAL: $498.17

AFTER

BEFORE

the color palette

Feeling stressed-out? Want to relax? There is nothing like a day at the spa to calm the senses. Our homeowners are spa devotees and wanted to bring the feel of a day spa into their backyard. Before beginning the project, I forced myself to spend an entire day at my favorite spa (just for research, mind you), International Orange on Fillmore Street in San Francisco. Stark white walls against dark, Brazilian cherry wood floors, black leather seating with faux mink throws, Egyptian cotton towels in the show-ers—this place is *to die for*. Once I emerged from my warm stone massage and facial, I felt up to the task of choosing fabrics,

textures, and colors for the deck project. Trying my best to mimic the look of this serene and peaceful spa on my meager budget, I chose white cotton fabrics, dark reddish wood tones, and a faux slate treatment for the floors. The result is a lush, tranquil refuge for our busy homeowners.

PAINT COLORS

Faux slate floor: Grout base coat: Navaho White, Kelly-Moore Standard
Slate gray tile: Knapped Flint, Kelly-Moore KM3831-3

OUTDOOR FURNITURE

Outdoor furniture is sold seasonally. If you wait until after the height of the season to purchase these items, you can save hundreds of dollars (or more) off the original retail price. Most home stores start these sales after the Fourth of July weekend and end them around Labor Day. (I purchased this teak set in August and saved 60 percent off retail.) Waiting till the last minute can save you the most money, but of course the selection will be picked over, and you may not be able to find everything you want.

Choosing the *correct* outdoor furniture is also important. When you're ready to start shopping for your deck or patio, do your homework and know which types of furnishings will work best for you and your lifestyle. There are basically five materials: aluminum, iron, wood, wicker, and plastic or resin. A hot new trend is wood pieces with metal accents for a sleek, modern look that still has the warmth of wood. However, looks alone should not determine which pieces you buy. You must decide how you're going to use the furnishings and how much effort you want to put into their upkeep. Where you live will also affect your choice: If you're near the ocean, avoid wrought iron, which can rust; if you're in a sunny climate, cushions are bound to fade, so invest in an attractive storage bin to hold these items when not in use.

Outdoor furnishings made from woods such as teak are a sophisticated look for any backyard. But you'll be applying sealers up to three times a year if you don't want them to develop the weathered gray look. Patio furnishings cast from resin—one of the most durable materials on the market—are the lazy man's friend: The most work you'll ever do is hose them down occasionally to remove dirt.

the details

Curtain rods were hung from the railings around the perimeter using standard curtain rod brackets screwed right into the wood canopy. Sheer cotton drapery panels were hung for privacy. Large stones can be placed at the foot of the drapery panels to secure them on windy days.

A glass-topped table gives the illusion of more space. On top sits a fountain made from a tin bucket and river rocks. This easy project adds the soft rippling sounds of water to the outdoor space. (Learn how to make your own fountain on page 100.)

NEW USES: **CHANDELIER ACCENTS**

The single bare bulb that was originally illuminating this deck was utilitarian at best. I wanted to add softer, more refined lighting. I found a simple black cast-iron chandelier ($40), but its overall appearance still seemed plain. So I added four crystal prisms to each arm of the fixture to imbue it with sparkle and interest. (Crystal prisms such as these can be purchased in bulk inexpensively on eBay.) In lieu of traditional shades, I used rattan decorative balls, found at most import and home stores. I used tin snips (scissor-like instruments used to slice metal—found at any hardware store) to remove a section of the rattan, then simply slipped the balls

Bring art into your outdoor room. This large, framed map was liberated from the guest room and now beautifully covers the bland beige wall. The plywood floor got a sophisticated makeover using paint. (See how we created this faux slate floor on page 101.)

Potted bamboo adds an exotic feel and is easy to care for. Speak with professionals at your local nursery about which plants will work best for your own patio and climate.

over the tear-shaped bulbs and secured them on the fixture's cylindrical metal base. For safety, make sure the bulb doesn't touch any of the rattan, and keep the wattage of the bulbs no higher than twenty-five watts.

Think of other creative covers for your own chandeliers. Tomato paste cans and soup cans make for unexpected and fanciful covers when you poke decorative patterned holes in them using a hammer and tin punch. Art-supply and craft stores sell a product called wire mesh: a flexible screen that comes in a variety of finishes such as copper, brass, and silver that can be molded into any shape and placed over the bulbs for a more organic alternative.

the projects

FOUNTAIN

A water feature can serve many functions in an outdoor living space. When water is in motion, it humidifies the surrounding areas, encouraging the growth of nearby plants and flowers. And its gurgling, melodious sounds can mask annoying city noises such as traffic and construction. I decided to bring a small tabletop fountain into the design to add another layer of organic style. Water pumps can be purchased inexpensively at most craft or garden-supply stores. Each pump is slightly different; follow the manufacturer's instructions.

Items you will need:

Reservoir for the fountain (I used an inexpensive tin bucket, but any water-tight container will do; pick one that suits your taste)

Filler (I chose smooth river rocks purchased from a nursery, but seashells, coral, or marbles could also be used)

Fountain pump

Water

Here's how you do it:

1. First fill the reservoir one-third full with the rocks. Place the water pump on the top of the pile.

2. Continue filling the container to the top with rocks, making sure to completely disguise the pump.

3. Simply fill with the water, according to the manufacturer's instructions, and turn on the pump. Some pumps will run on a battery, some with an electrical cord.

1

2

3

FAUX SLATE FLOOR

The homeowners wanted an elegant, up-scale design for their patio, so the shabby plywood flooring wasn't going to cut it. A stylish slate floor would be perfect for this spa look. But even if I had the budget for the extravagant material, the wooden structure of the deck would never hold the weight of so much natural stone. I decided to mimic the look of slate by using porch paint and some tape. Using porch paint is the key; regular latex paint will chip and peel over time. This can be a time-consuming project, but it's easy, costs less than $80, and looks realistic on wood or cement flooring.

Items you will need:

Porch paint, in shades of off-white and charcoal gray

Paint roller and tray

Chalk line

Painter's tape

Here's how you do it:

1. First, clean the flooring well with a mild detergent and let dry. Apply the off-white porch paint using a roller. This base coat will be your "grout" color.

2. Once the grout color has completely dried, make a grid using chalk lines. The grid pattern can be as large or as small as you would like; I chose 2×2-foot squares. Adhere painter's tape to the lines.

3. Paint over the tape with the charcoal paint.

4. To keep the grout lines looking crisp, remove the tape before the top coat has a chance to dry.

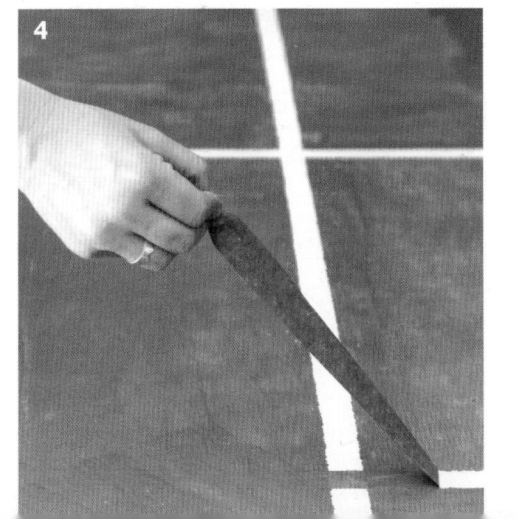

contemporary dining room

PROPORTION AND SCALE ARE TWO ELEMENTS OF DESIGN THAT SHOULD never be overlooked. And here's a secret: You may be overlooking proportion and scale issues right now and not even know it. Can you see your coffee table, or is it literally hidden by a huge overstuffed sofa and chair set? Is your dining table dwarfed to miniature proportion in your large dining room? If so, you may have a problem with scale and proportion. To remedy the situation, you first need to know what these terms mean. *Scale* is the size of a furniture piece or accessory in relationship to the entire room. *Proportion* is the relationship among the sizes of these individual pieces. In layman's terms, it's the philosophy of "Too big, too small, just right," just like the fairy tale. A large room with small or scant furnishings can seem like a cold and lonely cavern; a small room with oversize furniture or too many small pieces can feel claustrophobic. Getting it "just right" is the key, and here's some advice to help:

- USE COLOR. An effective way to fill space in a room is with color. Use rich, deep tones on your walls to create depth. Painting your ceiling the same rich tone as your walls will visually lower its height and make the space feel cozier. For smaller rooms, the old rule of sticking to pale colors is not necessarily true. As long as the color scheme of the space is monochromatic, you can use almost any color you wish, even red. It is the contrasting of colors that can make a small room feel smaller.

- MAKE IT BIG. To give a dinky window more presence in a large room, hang your curtain rod farther above and farther out the side of the window casing than is necessary. Choose large, flowing draperies and you end up with a "framing," a visual trick that designers have used for ages with fabulous results.

- DEFINE YOUR SPACE. Area rugs can be used to define and transition separate living spaces in large rooms. Choose identical patterns, or patterns that coordinate, to maintain balance.

the dilemma

They're not even *trying* here. What can I say about this poor, barren dining area, other than these gals need some help! Our occupants are a group of hip, style-savvy ladies in their early twenties who are right-fully ashamed of this sad, lonely room. They freely admit to the room's inadequacies and are ready for changes to make the space more stylish, warm, and user-friendly. (I wonder: Do they have to take turns eating in that one office chair?) We all eventually agree on a contemporary but wholesome look to replace the current minimalist theme they currently have.

THE GOOD NEWS

- The landlord says we can paint.
- The neutral-colored linoleum is in good condition.
- The wooden shelving unit is fabulous; it will work nicely into my design.

THE BAD NEWS

- The existing dining table is broken and too large for the space.
- The high contrast of the white and plum walls is too stark and jarring.
- The only seating is one office chair. Sad, really . . .
- The high ceilings make for a lot of wall space that will need to be covered.
- The one bare bulb on the ceiling makes the room even more depressing.

THE PLAN

I want to make this room as hip as the girls who live here by introducing modern fur-nishings and luminous color. The dining table and chair will be replaced with more appropriate items, and large art pieces will

AFTER

BEFORE

be hung from the walls to add interest and proportion—all for less than $500.

THE GRAND TOTAL: $495.16

The girls had tried to add some life to their dining room by painting an accent wall in a muted, deep plum tone. But against the stark white wall color of the rest of the room, this choice was a bit harsh. I wanted to tone down and soften the edges, so I chose colors from nature and a few of the major food groups: Chocolate brown and a new apple green accent wall make for a delectable palette. Wood and wicker furnishings add to the natural state of affairs, while silver accents add sparkle.

the color palette

NEW USES: **WINDOWS**

This sleek, contemporary sideboard with its glistening silver trim and transparent glass panel is a sophisticated addition to any dining room. However, it didn't start out this way; this elegant buffet was actually a shabby old storehouse window when I discovered it at an architectural salvage yard. It was covered in dust and slightly scuffed, but the glass wasn't broken and the frame was in good enough condition to restore. What sold me was the size; it would fit perfectly into the recessed wall space of the dining room, and its narrow depth wouldn't intrude into the room as much as a standard-sized buffet would. We simply washed the window with a mild detergent, sanded the chipped paint from the frame, and painted the wooden sections with a silver metallic paint. To affix it to the wall we used metal shelving brackets that were screwed into the window's wooden frame and then into the studs of the wall for support.

This salvaged window worked perfectly for my sideboard project; bifold doors or wooden shutters would have worked equally well.

When planning your own home projects, consider any object with a flat or semiflat surface that could be secured with screws and brackets. Railroad ties would add an old-world feel to a rustic, Tuscan-inspired room, whereas a salvaged Formica countertop could turn an average dining room into a retro '50s diner. Speak to someone at your local hardware store about the proper hanging tools for your job.

ARTY ALTERNATIVES

Wall decoration should be displayed in large scale for large rooms, but significant pieces of art can be a hard hit to the wallet. In this room, I chose collections of smaller pieces and presented them in uniform fashion to get a similar look. The key to success is to make sure all the individual pieces have a continuous theme or style. The wall hanging along the back is composed of identical components (details on page 109), while the prints are in matching frames with the same botanical theme and color palette. In your own home, consider displaying a collection of black-and-white family portraits in matching silver frames. Even a child's artwork can get a place of prominence when arranged along a wall in coordinating frames.

If you have a more limited art budget, there are ways to get a similar look for much less money using paint. Large, geometric shapes are easy to paint on your walls. One substantial form can be applied for a minimalist look, or you can create several different shapes in varying colors for a more dramatic look. For inspiration, visit local art museums or go online to see modern and mid-century artists such as Rothko, Reinhardt, and Mondrian.

the details

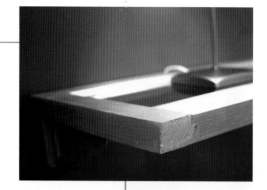

Asian-inspired buffet lamps cast a warm glow on diners from a cleverly repurposed sideboard. (See how some crackerjack recycling got us this new buffet on page 103.)

Finally the girls have a place to sit. These streamlined plastic-and-aluminum dining chairs were a bargain at $15 each (IKEA).

The groovy wall clock is actually painted on the wall with a modern, whimsical design that makes a functional item more fun. (Do it yourself on page 108.)

The existing wooden shelving unit was attractive but filled with mismatched barware and a globe that seemed to be lost amid a sea of shot glasses. I stashed all the barware in the kitchen and found the globe a new spot in the home office. Now the shelving houses a collection of wicker baskets, ceramic pots, and silver buckets—greenhouse accessories that enhance the natural theme and give a more tidy appearance.

The girls' old dining table was so massive they couldn't fit chairs around it (even if they'd had chairs!). The new, smaller table is a better size for the room, and it has a savvy secret: Its adjustable top can open to accommodate up to eight for dinner parties.

the projects

WALL CLOCK

Everyone needs a clock, but the digital LCD models can be so ugly. I wanted to make a fun and functional piece of art for the dining room. Wall clock kits can be found at most craft stores, but I found this one at Urban Outfitters (see "Resources," page 187); it had a touch more glam than the ones I saw at the craft store. The kit itself comes with colorful plastic biscuits that serve as the numbers for the clock. I didn't like the multicolored look for this project, so I decided to paint my own numbers using stencils.

Items you will need:

Wall clock kit

Acrylic or latex paint

Artist's brush

Number stencils

Painter's tape

Round template (such as a large platter)

Pouncer brush (a round sponge brush made especially for stenciling—can be found with the stencils)

Here's how you do it:

1. Unpack the clock kit and install the batteries according to the instructions.

2. Because it will be a rare case that you find a premade clock to match your decor, paint the clock with paint left over from the room for an identical match.

3. With the template as a guide, tape the stencils to the wall. Using the pouncer brush, apply the paint.

4. Attach the clock to the wall.

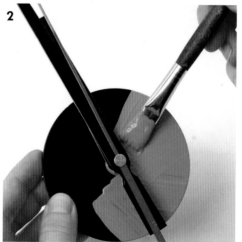

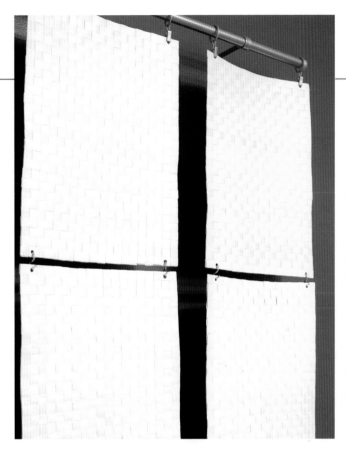

PLACE MAT ART

I love to tie food and food-related accessories into kitchen and dining-room designs to add a whimsical touch to these utilitarian spaces. In this room, I hung twenty place mats from a curtain rod to fill an empty wall. The curtain rod was hung using brackets and wall mounts, just as if you were hanging a window treatment. The result is a fun conversation piece. The simple basket-weave pattern of these mats adds texture and interest to the room without overpowering the space with too much color or pattern. You can find place mats in colors to match any decor; just make sure you pick a material that can be punctured with a hole punch for this project.

Items you will need:

20 place mats

Hole punch

Curtain rod

10 drapery clips

40 S hooks

Here's how you do it:

1. First, punch holes in all four corners of the place mats.

2. Next, attach a row of 5 mats to the drapery clips hanging from the curtain rod.

3. To form the chain of mats, slip the S hooks into the holes of the mats and attach more mats to the desired length.

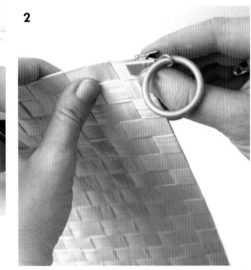

1

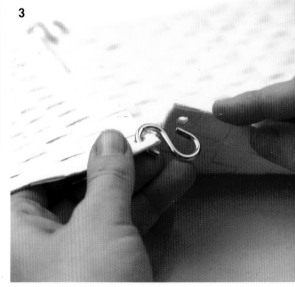

2

3

exotic rooms

These days you don't necessarily have to leave your zip code to get a well-traveled look for your home. Import stores have come a long way from the watered-down looks of yesterday, and the merchandise in the chain stores has become much more sophisticated. You can get a global look at domestic prices with these import shopping tips:

- **MIX IT UP.** Blend less costly items with treasured pieces for a harmonious design.
- **LESS IS MORE.** Take it easy when it comes to "themey" items. Strike a balance between kitschy and neutral pieces.
- **GET ON THE LIST.** Most family-owned, direct import stores will put you on a call list, which means they will contact you the minute a new container arrives from overseas. Ask to be put on your favorite stores' lists to ensure you get a head start on all the great buys.
- **GET INSPIRED.** Need inspiration? Peruse travel magazines and brochures, as well as the Internet, for authentic looks.

moroccan den

THE CONCEPT OF THE DEN HAS EXPLODED ONTO THE ARCHITECTURAL SCENE in the past few years. Whether you call it a family room, a rumpus room, or an entertaining area, the idea is the same: a room that's less stuffy than the formal living room, where you can let it all hang out. Functionality is the main thing to consider when decorating a den space. Think of how you plan to use the room and design around that.

- **SET THE MOOD.** Family entertainment is usually the main function. Will there be a television and stereo equipment? Most new homes offer built-in entertainment centers to house these appliances. If you live in an older home, you might consider an armoire or wardrobe to conceal all those cords and wires that can make a room look cluttered. When choosing the major furnishings, remember: You're not going to want to watch a two-hour movie in a stiff, upright chair. When shopping, think about your lifestyle and test drive the pieces. Plop into a sofa and squirm around in it a bit. Is this a comfortable place to lounge and eat popcorn?

- **MAKE IT KID FRIENDLY.** If you have children, you may want to consider a floor plan with an emphasis on the floor part. Children can take up a lot of space playing. Keep an area of your room open for speedways and fashion shows. Choose durable fabrics that will be easy to clean and will not show wear. Storage is a must for all the toys, so look for multipurpose furnishings that can serve as both storage and seating (benches and ottomans with inside storage are great options).

- **LET THE GOOD TIMES ROLL!** Love entertaining in your home, but are lacking the time or energy to prepare sit-down dinners? A den with comfortable seating and small cocktail tables can take the place of a fully appointed dining room.

the dilemma

Lois recently purchased a home near a college. In its former life, this house had served as rental property to generations of students. Years of keg parties and youthful indifference have left it in dire need of Design 101! Lois has decorated the other rooms with a warm mix of family antiques and rustic accessories, and the last area to be tackled is the bonus room. Although the space is currently being used for storage, Lois would like a den—a place where the family can lounge. A recently purchased ornate wooden floor screen is her inspiration piece, and she'd like to see the room refurbished in an exotic, Moroccan style.

AFTER

BEFORE

THE GOOD NEWS

- The room is huge (around 20 by 17 feet).
- The floors are hardwood, a perfect foundation for a rustic look.
- The ceilings are 9 feet high.
- There are three large windows, which bring in scads of natural light.
- I may be able to use certain existing pieces in the design, which means more bang for my budget.

THE BAD NEWS

- The paint color is straight out of a 1950s school cafeteria.
- The window treatments are held together with duct tape (literally).
- Those fabulous windows look out onto a dismal alley.
- There's no comfortable seating.

THE PLAN

The first thing that has to go in this room is the institutional aqua paint; I want to see rich adobe colors for the walls. The well-worn window shades will be the next to leave, but I'll need to find a new treatment that allows light to enter but obscures the terrible view. Seating is a major issue in this room, and we need comfortable pieces that will accommodate the entire family. Lois's wooden floor screen has just the right look for the Moroccan design she wants, but I don't think it's being displayed properly. I have plenty of ideas for turning this neglected back room into a Moroccan retreat for less than $500.

THE GRAND TOTAL: $497.50

the
color
palette

My inspiration was the dramatic landscape of North Africa, a land surrounded by white-capped mountains, the azure sea, and the caramel-hued desert. Marrakech has been described as the Red City because of the color of its buildings, which were built from the region's red sand. My goal for Lois's den is to bring in those earthy pigments and to give the illusion of a sun-drenched adobe hut. I chose hues in gold, burnt umber, persimmon, and mocha. The room had been painted a bright turquoise, and I decided to leave the blue tone on the ceiling, creating the illusion of an alfresco daytime sky. The walls were then painted gold and persimmon. Soft, cream-colored couches fill the room and add to the feeling of spaciousness.

PAINT COLORS

Gold: Hacienda Clay, Kelly-Moore KM3541-2
Latex glaze: Mocha, McCloskey (this premixed glaze can be found at most paint stores)
Persimmon: Prairie Island, Kelly-Moore KM4094-2

ARTWORK SCALE

There is so much going on in this room with textures, patterns, and color; I wanted to keep the artwork large and graphic to prevent the room from feeling congested. Even though the screens are ornate, their large scale keeps the room looking uniform. When choosing artwork for your own home, remember that in general, a few large pieces look better than an accumulation of smaller, mismatched items.

NEW USES:
CREATIVE TABLETOPS

I used an old door and a few baskets to serve as the buffet table in this room. What sold me on the door was its size and worn, rustic appearance; I purchased it at a salvage yard for $35, so the price couldn't be beat. A door is not the only object we could have used, however. Tabletops can be created from any semiflat surface: glass, painted plywood, salvaged marble or stone, even old Formica countertops. Legs can be purchased at any hardware store or can be fabricated from cinder blocks, books, or clay pots.

the details

Moroccan design involves lots of elaborate tile work. I created a similar look using a stamp ($2 at a craft store) and white paint.

I brought in natural elements to soothe the senses. The warm glow of candles and the fresh scent of lemons will add to the tranquil mood. The elaborate window treatment was fashioned from a fast-food give-away. (For details, see page 118.)

Much of Moroccan entertaining involves sitting low to the ground. I fashioned this buffet table from an old door I found at a salvage yard. I simply sat it atop three large baskets, which serve as the table's base. Pillows from the sofa can be used for seating when the table is being used for dining.

Lois's wooden floor screen was being ignored, all cramped in the corner of the room. I made it more of a focal point by disassembling it, painting it white, and hanging it on the wall. You can find screws at the hardware store with little hooks at the end. We screwed these into the studs of the wall and slipped the hooks into the carved openings of the screen.

This luxurious-looking sectional sofa is actually two inexpensive futons: a full-sized along the back wall, and a twin-sized down the side wall ($248 for both, IKEA). They'll provide comfortable seating for the whole family and can also serve as guest beds.

Pillows make the look in this room. They are cushy to sit on and add to the comfortable, casual feel. Most of the smaller ones were less than $6 each, which is why I could buy so many.

the projects

BURGER KING CROWN STENCIL

One day while driving my four-year-old daughter home from her favorite fast-food restaurant, I noticed how regal she looked in her newly acquired paper crown. Then it hit me: "Hey, I could use that!" She said I would need to get my own, so I did. From that day on, I have continued to find different uses for this unlikely design element. The first time was as a stencil in Lois's room.

Items you will need:

Burger King crowns

Pencil

Paint

Artist's brush(es)

Here's how you do it:

1. First, collect a few crowns. The restaurant will usually give you these for free if you ask, but it may request a small fee if you want a lot of them.

2. Outline the crown on your wall using the pencil.

3. Using the wall paint, color in the lines with the artist's brush. I will warn you: Depending on the size of your room, this can be a time-consuming project. Keep in mind that the result is supposed to look like a worn, hand-painted fresco. So don't get too caught up in making it look perfect. The mistakes will only add to the charm.

BURGER KING CROWN WINDOW TREATMENTS

I had a challenge with the windows: I wanted lots of natural light, but the alley view was less than attractive. I needed something that would allow light in but at the same time disguise the dismal landscape. Another hurdle was that I had used up my entire budget at this point. So bring in the fast-food crowns!

Items you will need:

Burger King crowns (depending on the number you will need, you may have to pay; I paid $6 for 50 of them).

Spray paint (we used off-white to match the window trim, but any color could work; avoid brushing on the paint because it doesn't dry quickly enough and the moisture will cause the cardboard to disintegrate)

Adhesive (we used rubber cement, which sticks well and can be removed easily; silicone is another option but it's less forgiving)

Scissors

Here's how you do it:

1. Spray-paint all the crowns off-white to match the moldings. Remember to paint both sides. You don't want your neighbors thinking you're nuts!

2. Apply the adhesive according to the manufacturer's instructions.

3. Line up the crowns and stick them to the window; you may need to trim the edges for a perfect fit. If your window gets southern exposure, the crowns may curl over time. Use extra adhesive to make sure they stay put.

2

3

mexican living room

ACCESSORIZING YOUR HOME CAN BE THE MOST DIFFICULT TASK IN INTERIOR design. Those who have the most trouble seem to fall into two categories. First there is the über-minimalist camp, consisting primarily but not entirely of single, straight men. This group doesn't know what to do, so they do nothing. They are mere survivalists in their own homes, implementing such MacGyver tactics as engineering entertainment centers from milk crates and plastic garbage ties. My husband fell into this category. Hopelessly design-challenged, he initially caught my eye with his impressive repurposing of an ice chest into a coffee table. Form and function, what a man . . .

The other category is the "Whoa, Nelly!" faction. Every flat surface in these homes is filled to overflowing with collections, books, frames, stuffed animals, and figurines. Styles and colors clash in a battle royale with no holds barred. I can appreciate these folks' enthusiasm; they just need to exercise some restraint to achieve a more peaceful home.

Composition, scale, and arrangement are not design concepts that come naturally to everyone. Here are a few tips to help both camps find a happy middle ground.

- **TAKE THE EASY WAY OUT.** Balanced arrangements are a simple and effective way to get started accessorizing, especially when a more formal atmosphere is the goal. Few rooms are completely symmetrical on their own, but symmetrical layouts and vignettes can add balance.

- **TAKE A FIELD TRIP.** You can learn more about proportion and scale in an afternoon at Crate and Barrel than I gleaned from an entire semester at design school. Large furniture chains hire professional stylists to arrange the vignettes in their stores to help sell product. Study the compositions on your next window-shopping trip for a professionally pulled-together look in your own home.

- **HIRE A PROFESSIONAL.** Many interior designers offer a "use what you have" consultation service. For a small one-time fee, they will come in and rearrange the items you already own in a more attractive manner. This is usually a quick process and can make a huge difference in your home.

the dilemma

Candida and Mario take enormous pride in their shared Mexican heritage. Cultural icons and ancestral symbols fill their spacious home. The conundrum is how to display these beloved items in a more organized manner. The current method is a bit chaotic, and so the visual impact of the individual pieces is diminished. The couple would like their living room to be more streamlined and orderly, a space that showcases their treasures and celebrates their culture.

THE GOOD NEWS

- The room is a nice size (15 by 19 feet).
- The hardwood floors are in good condition.
- Beamed ceilings, crown moldings, and a fireplace add architectural interest.
- Most of the existing rustic-pine furnishings can be used in my design, which will save money.

THE BAD NEWS

- The fireplace is not functional and the sooty brick facade is unattractive.
- There is no sense of symmetry or order in the layout.
- Too many small accessories scattered about is jarring to the eye.
- The contrast of the dark wall hangings against the white walls is too stark.

AFTER

BEFORE

THE PLAN

I want to wash the walls in a warm adobe finish to soften the room's hard edges. Next, we will eliminate all but the most treasured of the couple's possessions to give the space a more open, soothing feel. And the unsightly fireplace will need to be disguised in some way. My mission is to take a cluttered living room and turn it into a hot spot fit for a fiesta for less than $500.

THE GRAND TOTAL: $495.02

the
color
palette

Tropical fruits, desert sand, and sunbaked clay tiles were my inspiration for the color scheme for this room. I chose an adobe rust hue for the walls; we mixed the paint with a clear latex glaze and applied it to the wall with a rag in a random, circular motion to provide the textured look of stucco. Cool sage greens are carried throughout the room in window treatments and throw pillows. The white ceiling beams were given a more rustic appearance with a combination of woody brown tones (see page 126 for step-by-step instructions). Hot pink adds a touch of *¡Ay Carumba!* to the easygoing backdrop.

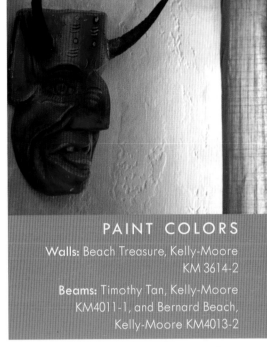

PAINT COLORS
Walls: Beach Treasure, Kelly-Moore KM 3614-2

Beams: Timothy Tan, Kelly-Moore KM4011-1, and Bernard Beach, Kelly-Moore KM4013-2

NEW USES: **BEER BUCKETS**

I found these snazzy Corona ice buckets while shopping at El Paso Import Co., a funky store in San Francisco that sells direct imports from Mexico and other parts of the world (see "Resources," page 187). I purchased the buckets impulsively; I had no idea where I would use them in this room, but they were so cool I knew they would fit in somewhere. They wound up as part of the altar we built on the mantel. Instead of ice and beer, they contain fresh bananas, and add a tropical feel. The height of the buckets alone was not right for the space, so I secured tin cups to the bases using a silicone adhesive. Terra-cotta plant pots would work well for a similar look.

HOME ALTARS

The Mexican home altar, a tradition that goes back to the Mayans, is usually associated with the Mexican Day of the Dead, or Día de los Muertos. This is a period of abundant celebration when the spirits of the dead return to visit loved ones, and altars are constructed to honor those who have passed. Photographs, candles, and the deceased's favorite foods are the cornerstones of these memorials.

Altars can serve solely as a holiday decoration, or they can become a yearlong expression of one's spirituality. For a more modern twist, mix a bit of the new with the traditional. Pair a Tom Waits album cover with a Buddha adorned in Mardi Gras beads. Nature lover? Arrange dried leaves, flowers, and stones in a simple wooden bowl with old photographs and poems. The individual items are yours to choose; creating a personal, sacred collection is the key.

the details

An old sombrero, a tropical plant, and a skeleton incense burner make for a festive vignette. Think about scale and proportion when displaying items in your own home: A few large pieces looks better than a scattering of small knickknacks.

Leopard print may not be a fabric traditionally connected to Mexican design, but it makes a strong statement paired with hot pink throw pillows in the new seating area. The wicker chairs were found scuffed and forgotten in the scratch-and-dent department at a discount furniture store ($14.95 each). A quick coat of touch-up paint and they're good as new.

The positioning of religious symbols with flickering candlelight creates an altar effect on the fireplace mantel. (For more information on traditional and not so traditional altars, see page 123.)

Reproductions of vintage Mexican movie posters were purchased from eBay for $20 each. Their large scale and bold graphic design lend color and interest. Colorful, patterned pillows add comfort and style to the plain white futon.

The scruffy fireplace facade was given a quick face-lift. (See how I mimicked the look of pressed tin on page 127.)

the projects

PAINTED BEAMS

The living room had a wonderfully detailed beamed ceiling, but the whitewashed beams created a more formal look than I wanted. To give them a more rustic appearance, I decided to use a dry-brush technique to mimic the look of worn pine. The process could not be easier, and you don't have to be an artist to get an authentic look.

Items you will need:

2 shades of brown paint, 1 at least 2 shades darker than the other

Two 2-inch paintbrushes

Paint rollers and trays

Roll of paper towels

Here's how you do it:

1. First, paint the beams the lighter of the two browns using the paintbrush or the roller. This may take more than one coat; allow each coat to dry thoroughly before applying the next.

2. Once the base coat has dried, dip the paintbrush into the darker brown paint. Wipe off most of the paint onto a paper towel until you have a mostly dry brush.

3. Gently skim the brush along the surface. Make sure your brushstrokes move in the same direction to get the most realistic look.

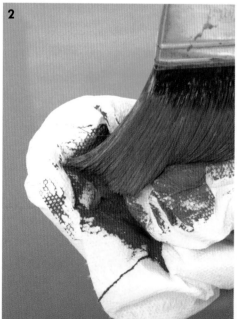

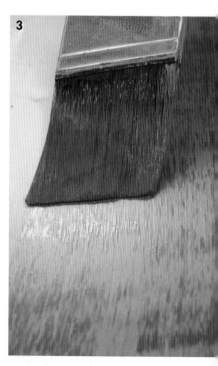

PRESSED TIN FIREPLACE

Stamped tinwork is a traditional Mexican folk-art form used by artisans to create decorative and religious objects. You can find examples of this craft on mirrors, picture frames, lanterns, and *nichos*, which are small metal keepsake boxes. I wanted the same look for the facade of Candida and Mario's brick fireplace. Not being a Mexican artisan myself, I would need to find a prefab product I could simply place over the top. I should remind you now that the fireplace in our case is nonworking—it had been sealed years earlier due to structural issues. This opens up the possibilities for me while looking for a suitable cover: Because there will be no fires in this fireplace, I am not limited to flame-retardant products. This being the case, I found what I was looking for in the wallpaper department of a hardware store—there's a vast selection of embossed wallpapers to suit any taste. This project is inexpensive and easy to reproduce. Just don't use it on a working fireplace or you may burn down the house.

Items you will need:

Measuring tape

Pencil

Several rolls of embossed wallpaper (depending on the size of your project)

Straightedge or scissors

Silver spray paint

Repositionable adhesive such as rubber cement or a low-tack spray adhesive

Here's how you do it:

1. Using the measuring tape and the pencil, measure and mark the wallpaper to fit the face of your fireplace. Cut out the wallpaper with the straightedge or the scissors.

2. Spray the wallpaper with the metallic silver spray paint. This process really brings out the detail in the paper.

3. Apply the adhesive to the back and place over the facade. You don't want to use a permanent adhesive on this project because if the paper is ever accidentally torn, you want to be able to replace it easily.

african lounge

BOYS' NIGHT OUT . . . AH, THE BACHELOR PAD. NEVER HAS ONE LABEL BEEN associated with so much mischief. Boys will be boys, after all, and they need a playground. Decorating these dens of iniquity can be a lot of fun because these guys are usually up for anything. Most men require only a recliner and a plasma TV for a happy home. But to all you lounge lizards who want to make your pad the most swingin' in town, here's some solid advice from a real live girl:

- NUDIE POSTERS ARE NOT ARTISTIC. This type of home decor is just not acceptable. You may think this "art" collection projects the image of a hep-cat playboy, but it's really saying "immature creepy guy" to female guests. Posters of any kind are generally in bad taste, but these are the pinnacle. If you simply must have some skin showing in your home, stick to the vintage Bettie Page pinup variety. Have a few small photos placed in sleek black frames for the most sophisticated look.

- KEEP IT CLEAN. A bunch of guys living together in one space can get dirty. If you can't keep the place clean yourself, consider pitching in and hiring a cleaning service to come every two weeks.

- A PLACE FOR EVERYTHING. For the public areas, shop for coffee tables and end tables with storage to house remote controls, playing cards, *TV Guides*, *protection*, whatever you may need at your fingertips. Avoid prefab entertainment units. These behemoths of the bachelor pad are seldom attractive and, because of their cheap construction, tend to sag over time. Shop for more creative options such as an antique trunk, armoire, or dining hutch to store your electronics.

- CONSIDER A SOFA BED OR FUTON. Those late-night parties can leave you with overnight guests. A convertible sofa or futon is the perfect crash pad.

the dilemma

Three wild and crazy guys need some design help with their new party pad. The area in question is the den, whose primary focus will be entertaining. The men complain that the space is too bright during the day and too dark at night. When they entertain, their guests inevitably wind up mingling in the cramped kitchen. They would like to have the den transformed into a hip, mellow gathering spot. One of the housemates is a collector of African art, and the decision has been made to emphasize this theme. Always up for a party, I'm excited to get started.

THE GOOD NEWS

- The larger furnishings are in good shape and can be salvaged.
- The brick wall adds architectural interest.
- The room is large (14 by 16 feet).

THE BAD NEWS

- The wall-to-wall carpet is dingy and will need to remain covered.
- The current area rug is shabby.
- The window treatments are old and dingy.
- The walls are clean but boring.

THE PLAN

I want to bring color and interest to the blank white walls using several paint colors and painting techniques. The guys also need a bar and better mood lighting. My goal is to give them all of this and more for less than $500.

THE GRAND TOTAL: $439.42

BEFORE

AFTER

the color palette

The brightly colored, intricately designed kente cloth of West Africa was my inspiration. These fabrics are used throughout the region in religious ceremonies and for clothing and headdresses. I chose to pull these vibrant, primary colors into the room using paint: apple green for the walls with gold and tomato accents. The black-and-white design of the mud-cloth tapestry adds contrast and interest. Search the Internet for African fabrics. Many companies will send you a sample swatch before you buy.

NEW USES: **KITCHEN ISLANDS**

This bar started out life as an unfinished butcher block island (IKEA, $79). I painted it black, and added a grass skirt to go with the African theme. The skirt, applied using a hot-glue gun, disguises the barware stored on the inner shelves.

LET'S GET THIS PARTY STARTED

The guys wanted a bar for their new lounge, so we created a funky, tiki-inspired landing pad for their guests. We made this one ourselves, but inexpensive and equally cool bars can be found in a variety of locations. Flea markets and estate sales are excellent resources for vintage '70s versions with fake wood paneling and leopard print insets. Have patience, however. The inconsistency of the inventory at these outlets can mean months of searching before you find any results. If you're in more of a hurry, try the Internet: eBay and Google listings feature bars for sale right away—the downside being that you may have to pay a large shipping fee if the seller lives in another part of the country.

the details

Round paper lanterns cast a soothing glow. Informal seating is created by scattering large pillows on the floor.

The wall of framed tribal masks carries the stripe from the back of the wall around the room and adds continuity to the space. (See how they were made on page 134.)

African sculpture makes for a lovely still life paired with a lively palm. (See how the planter was constructed on page 135.)

A swatch of cotton fabric with traditional African design is framed and used as artwork. At $3.99 a yard, this is the best buy in the room. Most fabric stores carry extensive varieties of internationally inspired fabric.

One of the roommates was using this boldly designed mud-cloth tapestry as a blanket on the sofa. It makes a much bolder statement as window treatments. I used drapery clips to hang the ornately designed fabric from the curtain rod.

Contemporary touches like this low-profile coffee table add balance and keep the African theme in check.

the projects

TRIBAL MASK ART

There's nothing more striking in an African-inspired room than a collection of traditional tribal masks. The challenge can come when trying to acquire this collection; authentic tribal sculpture can cost thousands of dollars. Import stores offer reproductions at reasonable prices, but I've found a way to get a similar look for even less money by using clip art and some imagination.

Items you will need:

Several African mask images (you can download them from clip art websites or find them at a library and make copies)

Scissors

Fancy paper (I found papyrus at an art-supply store; you could also use fabric with African designs for a bolder look)

Clear double-sided tape (or looped Scotch tape)

Picture frames with mats (these were $20 each, mats included)

Here's how you do it:

1. Cut the image out using scissors.

2. Secure the image to the paper with the tape.

3. Place the image into the picture frame, and you have instant art.

3

1

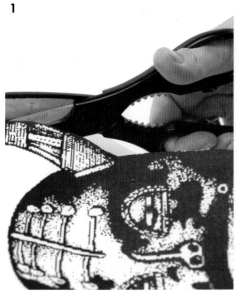

2

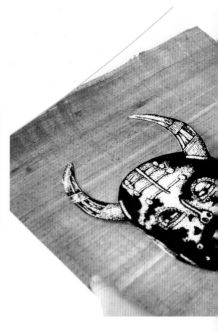

NATURE-SCAPE PLANTER

We had a terrarium in our living room when I was a kid. The whole idea of the tiny isolated environment with its own little climate fascinated me. I could sit and watch the mist form and drip down the edges for hours. (But, hey, I lived in the country; there wasn't much else to do.) I've got a project here that can give you that same glimpse into nature and make a plain old potted plant a little more interesting.

Items you will need:

Large glass vase with a simple shape

Variety of decorative rocks in different shapes, colors, and sizes (you can find these at any garden-supply store)

Plant (small palms, peace lilies, and orchids work well)

Potting soil

Here's how you do it:

1. Start layering the rocks in the vase. Begin with the largest rocks and get smaller as you approach the top. Stop when you're about two-thirds up the vase.

2. Next, place the plant into the vase, making sure all the roots are buried. Add the soil as needed. As a finishing touch, sprinkle a few of the prettier rocks on top of the soil.

asian retreat

OLD MEETS NEW: BLENDING MODERN, SLEEK FURNISHINGS WITH MORE rustic, timeworn pieces is a stylish way to add an eclectic balance to any space. Finding equilibrium is the challenging part. You need to step off the beaten path when combining styles, textures, and eras. Experimentation is essential and patience a must; this is not a style for the timid or quick-tempered. Here are a few tips to help you along the way:

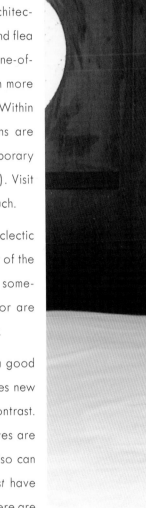

- **KNOW WHERE TO GO.** Architectural salvage yards, estate sales, and flea markets are the places to go for one-of-a-kind antique objects to mix with more modern furnishings. IKEA, Design Within Reach, and Scandinavian Designs are good resources for sleek, contemporary items (see "Resources," page 187). Visit import stores to add an exotic touch.

- **GET CONNECTED.** To keep an eclectic room from feeling disjointed, most of the objects in the room should have something in common. Scale and color are two important factors to consider.

- **STAY SAFE.** In the kitchen, it's a good idea to keep the major appliances new and bring in older accents for contrast. The older refrigerators and stoves are not only energy hogs but they also can be dangerous. If you simply *must* have the look of vintage appliances, there are several companies that make antique reproductions. From ranges to blenders, you can find just about anything your heart desires.

- **TRUST YOUR INSTINCTS.** If you love everything in your home, there will be a natural continuity. Be true to yourself, and you're sure to succeed.

the dilemma

The last child has left for college, and now it's time for this couple to start thinking about how they want to reclaim their home. The first room they'd like to conquer is the master bedroom. They would like to carry the ethereal, peaceful mood of their newly designed Japanese garden into the bedroom. They agree that the current hodgepodge of furnishings and accessories is neither attractive nor functional. Major changes will need to be made to achieve a more relaxed feel. The couple is excited about the new look, and I can't wait to get started.

THE GOOD NEWS

- The room is large (14 by 16 feet).
- The hardwood floors are in pristine condition.
- The French doors allow natural light to flood the space.
- The newly landscaped Japanese garden is the perfect inspiration for my design.

THE BAD NEWS

- The walls are drab and lifeless.
- The bedding is dated and worn.
- There's not adequate storage for clothing.
- There are dining chairs in here. What's up with that?

THE PLAN

I plan to dress the walls in rich color and texture using a rag-rolling technique. Next, I'll be exchanging the white princess furniture for darker, more rustic pieces, and I'll upgrade the dated, worn bedding. My ultimate goal is to transform an old-fashioned, jumbled bedroom into an exotic retreat for less than $500.

THE GRAND TOTAL: $488.48

AFTER

BEFORE

the color palette

When I sat down to discuss color schemes with the homeowners, they immediately expressed an interest in a traditional palette of Chinese red and black lacquer. The couple are followers of Eastern philosophy and, with the new addition of a Japanese garden, they assumed this classic Asian look would complement their new surroundings. But I feared this daring color combination would be too stark an environment for this laid-back couple. Sometimes we can be impulsively drawn to a style in a magazine or a designer shop, but living with it day after day can be another matter. It's my job to ensure that each makeover is well loved years after I'm gone. After much discussion, we all agreed to stick with the same basic idea but soften it up a bit. The result: A soothing, persimmon glaze was rag-rolled on the walls for warmth and texture; a glossy burnt umber was chosen for the larger furnishings. Chartreuse and gold accents add sparkle and interest to our new, earthy palette.

NEW USES: **FINE PAPER**

My goal was to bring some authentic Asian art into this space, but on my small budget I was going to have to get creative. While shopping one day, I discovered a family-owned handmade paper store that specialized in traditional Japanese design. I spent a good part of the afternoon perusing the stacks and stacks of delicate papers with intricate designs, ranging from subtle to bold. A glistening sheet with a muted watercolor background and Japanese characters written across in black and gold ink caught my eye. It was stunning, and at $20 I couldn't resist. If your town doesn't offer such a specialty shop, there are many alternatives. Look on the Internet, or consider framing a swatch of printed fabric, foreign newspaper print, or even takeout menus for a cheap alternative to real artwork.

DON'T JUDGE A VANITY BY ITS COVER

One of Mrs. Benson's contributions to the master bedroom was an old, slightly worn princess vanity she'd had since college. It had been a useful piece of furniture to her for all these years, but she had to admit its appearance didn't suit her anymore, and the broken mirror was an eyesore. She assumed it would be one of the furnishings sacrificed to the junk pile. Initially, I agreed. Until I took a good look and discovered that the "bones" were still in excellent shape. We removed the cracked mirror and painted the vanity and bench a dark, chocolate brown to match the new armoire. A new mirror was hung above, and the bench was re-covered in a shiny chartreuse silk. Now what was old is new again. Take a look at some of the old furnishings in your own home. Could any of them use a face-lift? Paint is cheap and can make a huge difference.

the details

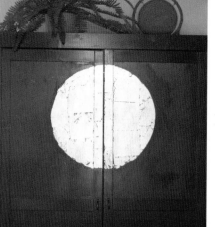

An unfinished armoire was purchased for much-needed clothes storage. (See how we gave it some Asian flare on page 142.)

A bamboo stool and wooden platter give a small sculpture more presence and scale. Garden shops and import stores are superb resources for bamboo accessories.

The homeowners' existing furniture received a makeover with a coat of dark brown epoxy paint. The epoxy paint contains an adhesive allowing it to stick to any surface.

The framed artwork cost less than $45. (Get details on page 139.) As for the headboard, we taped off a rectangular area above the bed before the walls were painted. Once the walls dried, we simply removed the tape and, voilà, a faux headboard. The center bronze strip was added using the same taping technique and metallic acrylic paint.

Candlelight flanks a modern round mirror.

Recurring geometric shapes keep this room looking modern and fresh.

the project

GOLD-LEAFING

Traditional Chinese cabinets are typically finished in a shiny black or red lacquer and have a large round, brass medallion on their doors. I wanted the same look for the Bensons' bedroom but had the budget only for an unfinished pine armoire. We first painted the chest using a dark brown, epoxy-based latex paint for extra shine and durability. The rest of the transformation was made using a gold-leafing kit. Be warned: This project is messy and can try even the most enlightened soul. But if you hang in there, the results are amazing.

Items you will need:

Round template (I used a large wooden platter)

Craft paper

Pencil

Scissors

Painter's tape

Spray adhesive

Gold-leafing kit (can be found at any art-supply store)

Several inexpensive artist's brushes with soft tips

Here's how you do it:

1. First, draw the circular pattern for your medallion on the craft paper using the pencil and the template. Cut out the pattern using the scissors.

1

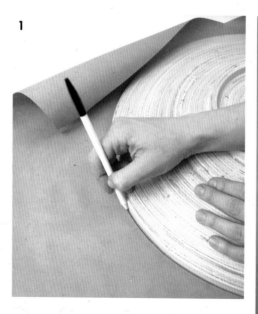

2

2. Next, adhere the pattern to the chest using the painter's tape. Spray the adhesive onto the surface. To ensure you end up with a perfect circle, make sure not to get any of the adhesive underneath the paper pattern. Cover the entire area evenly.

3. Remove the paper and apply the gold leaf by laying the sheets of gold leaf on the sticky area and gently pressing them into place with the brush. The gold leaf is terrifyingly fragile and will stick to your fingers if you're not careful. Use its enclosed paper backing to help place the sheets. Once the sheet of gold leaf has been placed, you can't move it around. If you wind up with open spaces, go back and fill them in later with more gold leaf. Don't get too particular about this project or you will go insane. Just keep telling yourself that the mistakes make it look handmade and more special. That's how I got through it.

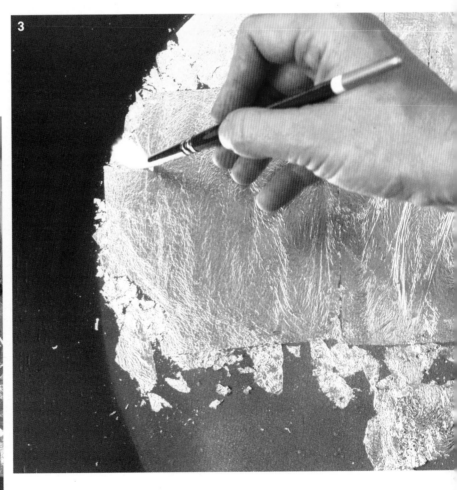

pad thai

THE FIRST APARTMENT: NOTHING CAN COMPETE WITH THE THRILL OF moving into your first place. But with so many decisions and so little cash, the process of getting started can seem overwhelming. It's easy to get swept away in the excitement and make impulsive purchases that can result in buyer's remorse. Save yourself a lot of money and grief by making a plan and sticking to it:

- KEEP IT REAL. Get your priorities straight and create a budget. Rent, utilities, food, car payments, insurance, gas, and savings all take precedence over that cute shag rug you spotted at the import store. Seek advice from family members or other trusted adults about how much you should be saving for necessities. Only *disposable* income should be used for luxury items. And, yes, the shag rug is a luxury; wear socks around the house until you can afford it.

- FREE IS GOOD. At a time when you may not be certain of your style anyway, invest as little as you can on furnishings. Instead, make treasure from another man's trash. Check out the classified ads or call your city to find out when bulk trash days occur. People are always throwing or giving away furniture. It may not be exactly what you want, but at least you will have a place to sit until you can afford something better.

- CONSIDER A FURNISHED APARTMENT. This option may take some of the fun out of your first foray into independence, but it will also reduce the stress involved with furnishing it. And remember, you don't have to stay there forever. This can be an enlightening time, a period to educate yourself about style and get a real taste of what things cost. Then when you're ready to move in to your next apartment, you'll be one step ahead of the game.

the dilemma

Wendy loves to travel. Since leaving college, she has extensively toured both South America and Asia. Now she's home and in her first real apartment. The years of traveling have been good for the soul but bad for furniture acquisition: Her worldly possessions consist of a mattress and box springs, a small wooden table, and two backpacks worth of clothes. My aim in this room is to give her some practical storage and bedding solutions while keeping the mood reminiscent of her traveling days.

THE GOOD NEWS
- The landlord says we can paint.
- The carpet is in good shape.
- The ceilings are high, and the room is a nice size (13 by 14 feet).

THE BAD NEWS
- Other than the mattress and box springs, there's nothing to work with.
- There's no closet, so I have to find alternative storage options.
- The bedding is in bad condition. It will all need to be replaced.
- There are no window treatments, and privacy is an issue.

THE PLAN
First apartments can be so drab. I plan to introduce rich colors and textures to the walls using paint. I'll provide window coverings for privacy, and add romance to the space by creating a headboard and a luxurious canopy to Wendy's existing mattress and box springs. Storage will be brought in to house her clothes. My goal is to turn a dull little room into a lush, exotic retreat for less than $500.

THE GRAND TOTAL: $475.62

AFTER

BEFORE

the color palette

I found this lightweight cotton throw while perusing an artists' market. I loved its exotic animal detail and rich color scheme. And, at $9, it was perfect for my budget. I used this throw as inspiration for the walls' muted lavender hue. Once the paint had dried, a bronze glaze was applied with a rag in a random, circular motion to provide the most texture. The result is an earthy feel with specks of sparkle as the light hits the walls. Furnishings in a deep cherry finish add contrast and warmth.

NEW USES: **PLANT STANDS**

Our Buddha seemed lost on the large-scale chest alone, so I wanted to find a small pedestal on which he could sit. What I found was a mobile plant stand in the gardening department of a hardware store. These are intended to be placed under large, heavy plants, so they can be easily moved. It was the perfect size and height for our more mystical needs, so I snatched it up. Two large pillar candles were added for effect.

Sculptural items often look best when placed on a pedestal of some sort. In our case, we could have opted for a stack of books on Asian religion and Buddhist philosophy, a deep glass casserole dish filled with sand, or even a small wooden footstool.

FOR THOSE WITHOUT A GREEN THUMB

I remember the artificial flower arrangement my grandmother had on her dining table for at least twenty years: enormous, orange plastic petals with avocado green and harvest gold accent flowers of unknown origin. She would take it out in the backyard and hose it down once a week to clean it. Fake greenery has come a long way since then. The grassy plants I used in this room were purchased for $3 each and have a realistic look and texture. You can fool your guests into thinking you have a green thumb if you heed a few tips:

Stay away from perfectly composed silk arrangements. They look dated and stale. Worse yet are those variegated ivy/pothos hanging plants everyone seems to have. During the 1980s, approximately eighty-seven million of these atrocities were sold in brass buckets to everyone in the United States. They are as tacky as white shoes after Labor Day. Get rid of them.

Just about everyone loves the elegant look of an orchid. But if you're like me, the poor plant would not have a chance at survival. (My husband hums "The Funeral March" every time I come home with a live plant.) I get the same look in my home by faking it. Invest in a nice strand of artificial orchid blossoms. Pier 1 Imports and Z Gallerie are excellent places to find more upscale blooms (see "Resources," page 187). Next, go to your local nursery and ask to see a selection of "hard to kill" plants. Choose a leaf shape that resembles the orchid's (I have used bromeliads and certain varieties of mother-in-law tongue with fantastic results). Stick the fake orchid into the pot with the live plant and, with minimal upkeep, you've got a fabulous year-round accent.

the details

A silky canopy cloaks the bed and reflects light from the overhead fixture. (See how easy it was to install on page 151.)

Wall sconces were substituted for table lamps. The choice clears up the tabletops for additional storage. The lights were attached to the wall using wall mounts found at any hardware store.

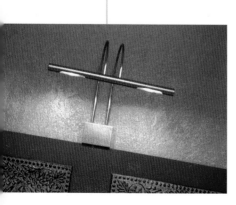

A picture light is repurposed as a reading light. We mounted it behind our home-made headboard using mounting screws. (See how the headboard was constructed on page 150.)

Heavy canvas draperies will provide privacy at night; silky sheers will keep prying eyes out during the day but will still admit daylight. A four-drawer cherry chest keeps all of Wendy's clothes organized, while Buddha sits on an unexpected platform. (See details on page 147.)

Wendy's small bathroom lacked adequate storage. I added wall hooks in the bedroom for towels and robes. A $10 folding chair makes for a novel plant stand.

My inspiration piece was this ethnic cotton tapestry, simply folded across the foot of the bed for interest.

the projects

CEILING TILE HEADBOARD

Most of the budget in this room was spent on big-ticket items such as the chest of drawers and the night tables. The simple mattress and box springs cried out for a headboard, but the solution would have to be super-cheap. I decided to create a headboard from tin ceiling tiles and a piece of fiberboard (on eBay you can find reproduction tiles inexpensively). These new tiles have handy hangers on the back for easy installation.

Items you will need:

Fiberboard or plywood cut to desired size (you want the width to be the same as your mattress; the height is up to you)

Spray paint (I picked a rich brown tone to coordinate with the night tables)

Wall mounts and screws

Screwdriver

2 or 3 ceiling tiles, depending on the size of your bed

Here's how you do it:

1. First, paint the fiberboard in a ventilated area.

2. Next, attach the painted board to the wall above your mattress using the wall mounts and the screws.

3. Insert the mounting screws into the wood and hang the ceiling tiles from their hangers.

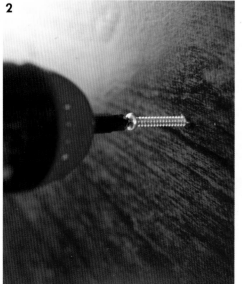

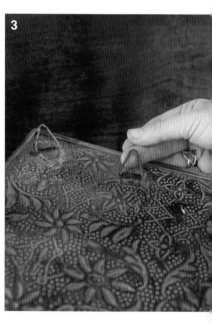

CANOPY

To give the mattress and box springs more presence, I built a simple canopy from a silky sheer panel and curtain rods. This is an easy project with stunning results.

Items you will need:

4 ceiling hooks

Drill

4 lengths of chain

2 curtain rods the width of your bed

1 sheer drapery panel

Here's how you do it:

1. Insert the ceiling hooks above the four corners of the bed according to the manufacturer's instructions. Loop the chain lengths and hang them from the hooks. Run the curtain rod through the sheer and place the ends of the rod into the chain loops.

2. Drape the end of the sheer over the curtain rod at the foot of the bed.

children's rooms

To me, there is nothing more rewarding than decorating children's rooms. Watching their little faces light up with excitement when they see their new rooms for the first time makes all the effort seem like child's play. If you're anticipating the arrival of your little one, choosing a crib and bedding can be a nice distraction from pregnancy nerves. If your youngster has a mind of his or her own (like mine), you may end up merely indulging demands for the latest Spider-Man or princess decor. Whatever the case, there are a few things you should know before getting started:

- **BE SAFE.** Always check for recalls on any children's furnishings, bedding, or toys. You can get this information at the U.S. Consumer Product Safety Commission (www.cpsc.gov).

- **CREATE LONGEVITY.** Pick a design that will grow with your child. Your baby is going to get older, and that baby sweet pea theme is going to embarrass him in front of his soccer buddies.

- **KEEP THEMES IN CHECK.** It's easy to get carried away and end up with a nursery that looks like a gift shop in an amusement park. Intersperse more neutral pieces with the themed items to achieve a balanced look.

- **PUT DAD TO WORK.** If you're pregnant, have Dad paint the room. Water-based latex paints have not been proven to cause any prenatal damage, but why take the chance?

- **HAVE FUN.** It's a kid's room, after all.

pretty in pink nursery

SHOPPING FOR BABY FURNISHINGS IS A FUN WAY TO PREPARE FOR THE ARRIVAL of a new family member. But don't get blinded by all the cuteness and forget about utility in the space. A nursery has so many functions: sleep zone, changing room, storage facility, playground, and library are just a few. And remember, you'll be spending almost as much time in the room as the baby will, so it should be comfortable and appealing to you as well. (Wait till he or she starts *teething*; you'll pace a groove in the floor.)

Ergonomics is the science of furniture design, intended to maximize productivity by reducing operator discomfort. Enlightenment in this area will save you many a backache:

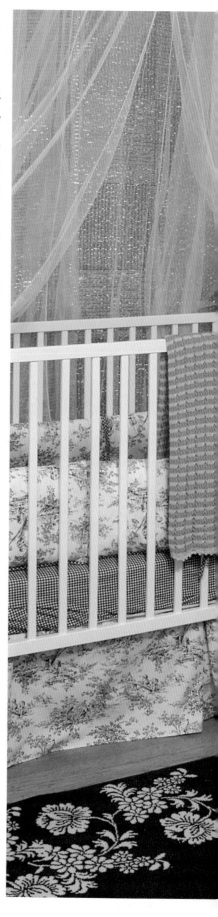

- SIZE MATTERS. Make sure changing tables and work surfaces are the right height. You may not notice at first, but having a surface even a few inches too high or too low can make handling a baby uncomfortable for you—and the baby.

- GET A HANDLE ON IT. Babies are very squirmy; you'll need to keep diaper-changing items close at hand so you can keep the other hand on the escapee.

- MAKE STORAGE COUNT. If your baby is as messy as mine were, keep clothes readily available in locations that don't make you bend over all the time. There were days when I might change my baby's clothes a half dozen times. You don't want to be stooping down or up on tiptoe to reach these items so often.

the dilemma

There's a new kid in town, which means it's officially time to change this cramped guest room into a nursery for baby Melia. From the looks of the rest of the home, I get the feeling her mom, Cary, will be leaning toward a feminine look. Main areas of the cottage are decorated with a dazzling mix of vintage crystal, candles, floral needle-point pillows, and worn, painted antiques. As for Melia's room, a stunning white-washed crib with black-and-white toile bedding has already been purchased. This will create a substantial foundation for my design. At her baby shower, Cary received an exquisitely detailed ballerina tutu for her daughter. She hopes we can use the tutu in the design. Wait till she finds out I plan to build the entire room around it!

AFTER

BEFORE

THE GOOD NEWS

• The room has remarkable architectural interest. Detailed crown moldings and Victorian light fixtures will add to the feminine vibe.
• Large windows provide soft, natural light.
• The homeowners have already purchased the crib and the bedding—generally, the most expensive items in a nursery.

THE BAD NEWS

• There's too much furniture in this room.
• The plain white walls are dull.
• The one lamp is too small and doesn't provide enough light.
• The current color scheme is lifeless.

THE PLAN

I will use the ballerina tutu as inspiration and bring in lots of pink to satisfy Mom's desire for an ultra-girlie nursery. The shabby-chic theme from the rest of the home will be carried into the nursery and the furnishings rearranged to best utilize the space. I plan to turn a cramped guest room into a nursery fit for a princess—for less than $500.

THE GRAND TOTAL: $485.12

the color palette

Melia's mom is a pretty hip mama, so I wanted to bring in a slightly more fashionable look than you might expect for an average nursery. My inspiration for the color scheme was vintage Chanel: The slightly muted pink against the high contrast of black is just so Jackie O. All of the large furnishings and window coverings were kept a soft creamy hue to give the room a more spacious feel. The black-and-white toile bedding adds yet another layer of elegant, feminine style.

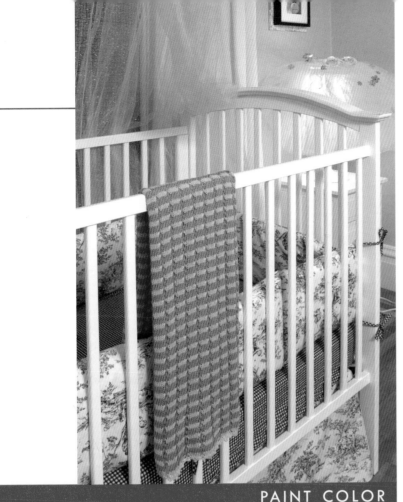

NURSERY FLOORS

It's always nice to have a soft place for the baby to crawl. I used a plush, synthetic-weave area rug to cover the cold hardwood floors. Here are some things to consider when purchasing floor coverings for your nursery:

- Make sure your rug is the right scale for the room. In an average-sized room, if more than three feet of flooring shows around your rug, then you need a larger one. Rugs that are too small will appear dwarfed and won't supply your little one with enough soft space for crawling.

- The baby will be playing on this rug, and eventually you may be changing him there when he gets too fidgety for the changing table. Choose floor coverings that are not only soft but also easy to clean, such as olefin or nylon.

PAINT COLOR
Desert Bloom, Kelly-Moore KM3668-1

NEW USES: ANTIQUE TIN CEILING TILES

I love antique tin tiles. They are almost exclusively a North American craft and were originally manufactured as an inexpensive substitute for the more costly carved-plaster ceilings found in Europe. Now you can find them at just about any architectural salvage yard. Back in the day, they were almost always painted a light color such as white or ecru. But over the years they rust and the paint wears away a bit, making for a wonderfully worn piece that adds charm to any home. I added them to the artwork in our nursery to soften the edges of the rather modern frames, but their uses don't end there. I have made headboards (see Ceiling Tile Headboard on page 150), window valances, even place mats out of these beautifully designed tiles. Alone they can be hung on a wall to add Victorian grace to modern homes that lack crown moldings and window detail. One thing to be aware of is lead paint. If you have concerns—perhaps your tiles may come in contact with food or children—there is an abundance of reproduction tiles on the market. They are brand-new; they just look old. You can find a vast supply on eBay with loops already applied to the backs for hanging.

the details

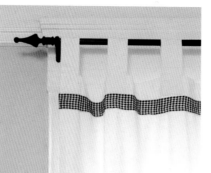

Have some tired curtains that need a lift? I added black-and-white gingham ribbon to existing drapery panels for more interest. The ribbon was attached to the panels using an adhesive iron-on tape found at any fabric or craft store. The result is a tailored, custom look. And it's so easy—you don't have to sew a single stitch!

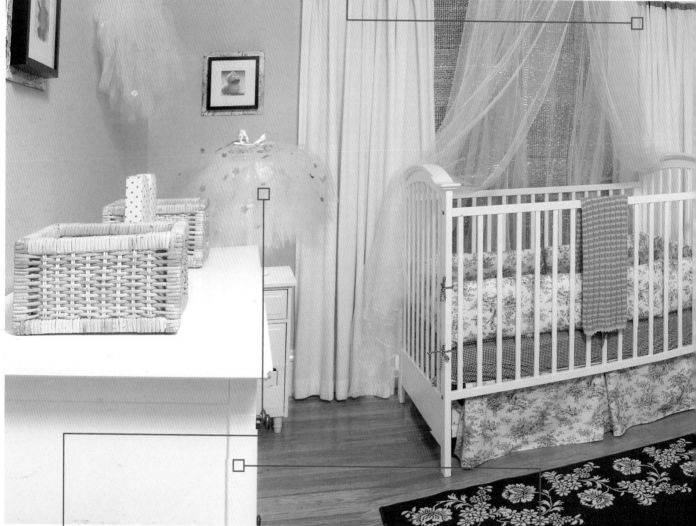

I made lamp-shade covers inspired by Mom's favorite baby item: the tutu. (Full details on page 161.)

This room desperately needed storage. A large wooden dresser was brought in for all of the baby's clothes. Sturdy with timeless detail, this dresser will not only last through Melia's teen years, but she may be dragging it off to her first apartment as well. Estate sales and flea markets are wonderful resources for large furniture pieces, but you have to be careful of what you're buying. Test your fabulous find for sturdiness and make sure the drawers slide easily before you take it home.

I've been known to pillage other rooms in the home for my designs. I spotted this rocking chair on the front porch and decided to steal it away for the nursery. Mom and Dad will forgive me the first night they need it. A coordinating cushion was added for comfort.

The teddy bear is the official mascot of the nursery. (To see how I made this one, check out page 160.)

Think outside the toy box when choosing storage options for your child's room. A nylon organization rack is now home to all of Melia's little furry friends. Inexpensive and easy to clean, the rack is a clever way to stash those playthings. We hung the rack on the wall using standard wall mounts purchased at the hardware store. Check out the organization/container section of your local superstore for storage solutions and fasteners.

the projects

TEDDY BEAR TOPIARY

I first made one of these topiaries as a centerpiece for a girlfriend's baby shower. It was such a hit with the girls that I decided to share the idea. It couldn't be easier to make and is a great conversation piece.

Items you will need:

Styrofoam balls: different sizes for the head and body; even smaller ones for the arms, ears, and snout

Toothpicks

Green moss

Floral pins

Dried flowers

Hot-glue gun and glue sticks

Stick (I chose bamboo)

Flowerpot

Floral foam

Here's how you do it:

1. Using the Styrofoam balls, make a bear shape. Your smallest styrofoam balls will have to be cut in half to resemble the arms, ears, and snout. Assemble the pieces using the toothpicks.

2. Next, attach the green moss all over the bear shape using the floral pins. Don't be stingy with the pins—the moss is very "loose" and needs to be well secured.

3. Add eyes, a nose, and buttons by hot-gluing dried flowers.

4. Once you've completed your bear, shove the stick up his bum (ouch!). You will now need to secure him in the flowerpot. Tightly place the floral foam into the flowerpot. Now insert the other end of the stick into the foam. Extra moss can be used to disguise the foam. You can add ribbons, bow ties, aprons . . . anything to give your bear its own personality.

1

2

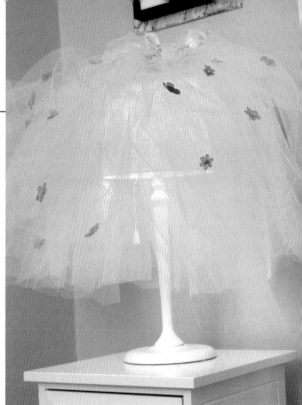

TUTU LAMP SHADES

Cary received a ballerina tutu for her daughter at her baby shower and wanted to incorporate it into the new room design. After all, what little girl doesn't feel like a princess in a tutu? I was trying to think of a way to use it when it dawned on me: lamp shades! Chic children's shops across the country sell exquisite tutus. You could simply buy one of those and attach it to any lamp shade. (Ironically, most lamp shades and a child's waist seem to be about the same size. Who knew?) However, you may be spending anywhere from $50 to $100 each on these custom items. I've found a way to get the same look for much less money; it doesn't even take that much work.

Items you will need:

Lamp with shade

Tutu (these can be found at dance shops; the ones I used were $11 each)

Pretty ribbon (preferably wired)

Hot-glue gun and glue sticks

Silk flowers (these can be found at rock-bottom prices on eBay)

Here's how you do it:

1. Start by pulling the tutu over the lamp shade. Leave an allowance at the top for your ribbon.

2. Next, tie the ribbon around the top; this will mimic the waistband of the tutu. You will probably need to secure the ribbon with a touch of the hot glue.

3. Last, fill in the gaps with the silk flowers. You don't want any of the lamp shade to show. I even glued a few smaller flowers onto the skirt to add depth.

For safety reasons, make sure no fabric is touching the lightbulb—or even placed *above* the lightbulb. Keep the wattage at 40 watts or below.

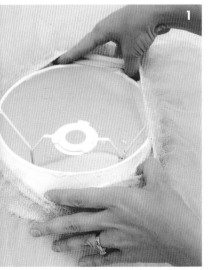

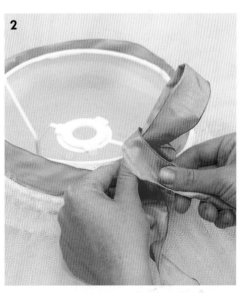

cowpoke nursery

DECORATING A CHILD'S ROOM CAN BE ONE OF THE MOST DIFFICULT DESIGN challenges in your home. It's tempting to buy all the cute little Bob the Builder and Sponge-Bob bedding sets you see at the children's stores, but themes fade fast. Unless you want to purchase an entire roomful of accessories each time your child discovers a new favorite show, it's best to stick to the basics. The walls, the bedding, and the flooring should remain a fairly neutral tone: Cream, tan, green, blue, and pink are traditional kid's-room colors that will stand the test of time. You can change the smaller accessories as your child grows and his tastes change. Consider these other practical tips when designing your child's room:

- KEEP IT CLEAN. Kids are impressively dirty. Make sure all of the paint finishes are washable and fabrics are machine washable. Keep storage within a child's reach so he can have no excuse for not keeping his room tidy.

- MAKE ROOM FOR PLAY. Kids, especially little boys, love to play on the floor. Reserve some floor space for racetracks and runways. Most children's stores sell a version of the "City Streets" area rug—it's usually pretty cheap and the boys go *nuts* for it. Easels and chalkboards are a fun way to get your kids' creative juices flowing (and will usually divert their need to draw on the walls).

- RECYCLE. Consider purchasing pre-owned furnishings. Thrift and consignment stores are excellent resources. Check the yellow pages or online for consignment stores specializing in children's clothing and furnishings. Trust me, after three months, it's all going to look broken in anyway.

the dilemma

For almost two years, Makhi has slept in a crib in his parents' room. He's becoming a big boy now and needs some space to call his own. His parents have chosen a spare bedroom and need help decorating. Mom tells me Makhi visited his first rodeo a few months back and became obsessed with all things cowboy, so she would like to see a rodeo roundup theme.

THE GOOD NEWS

- The room is large (13 by 13 feet).
- The hardwood oak floors will incorporate beautifully into a Western room.
- The existing antique chest has a rustic quality that will make a nice addition to my design.

THE BAD NEWS

- The only storage containers for Makhi's toys are unattractive milk crates that are difficult for the toddler to reach.
- There is no lighting.
- The walls are plain and scuffed.
- There are no window treatments.

THE PLAN

Makhi needs a big-boy room. I plan to discard the lonely crib mattress lying on the floor and get him a new bed with frame. The walls will be dressed in denim (perfect for a little cowpoke), and Western-themed furnishings and accessories will fill this cold, empty space—all for less than $500.

THE GRAND TOTAL: $385.17

AFTER

BEFORE

the color palette

This room desperately needed color. Since Makhi's mom wanted a Western theme, I decided to use colorful Mexican blankets as bedding and window treatments; their vibrant, primary tones add punch. And since every cowboy needs a good pair of blue jeans, faux denim glaze finish on the walls really sells the theme. This technique takes some experience to perfect, so it's a good idea to start on a practice board before you hit the walls. The secret is using good tools: Ralph Lauren offers excellent denim-weave brushes and rollers, as well as detailed manuals for this and other faux techniques.

PAINT COLOR
Piece of the Sky, Kelly-Moore KM3252-2

NEW USES: PACKAGING LABELS

This room needed so many furnishings that art became a low priority. But while searching the Internet for inspiration, I stumbled upon vintage vegetable crate labels. These intricately designed labels were used not only to identify the veggies and their growers but also as eye-catching advertising, and many of the California growers' labels used cowboys and Western art. The growers ceased production of the labels during the '50s, but even though they have become hot collectibles, you can find originals or less costly reprints at flea markets or on the Internet. I quickly found more than I needed on eBay. They were framed in simple black wooden frames, and for less than $30 we've got a wall of art.

Don't stop at vegetable labels. Vintage winery labels could add sophistication to a kitchen, a dining room, or a wine cellar. Many of the old fruit and cigar crate labels have a kitschy charm that would work with any retro decor.

INTERNET SHOPPING

I do as much shopping from my computer as I do out in the real world, maybe more. (This nursery is a good example: The Mexican blankets, the iron stars, the horseshoe hooks, the stuffed cow, the framed art . . . all from eBay.) In one sitting, you can order flowers for your mom in Florida, plan a vacation, buy stocks, and watch videos. However, this relatively new industry has its pitfalls. To make sure your transactions are secure, follow some simple cyber-savvy tips (from www.ftc.gov/index.html):

Shop with companies you know. Anyone can set up shop online under almost any name.

Keep your password private. Be creative when you establish a password, and never give it to anyone. Avoid using a telephone number, a birth date, or a portion of your Social Security number. Instead, use a combination of numbers, letters, and symbols.

Pay by credit or charge card. If you pay by credit card online, your transaction will be protected by the Fair Credit Billing Act. Under this law, you have the right to dispute charges under certain circumstances and temporarily withhold payment while the creditor is investigating them. In the event of unauthorized use of your credit card, you generally would be held liable for only the first $50 in charges.

the details

Always point a horseshoe up so your luck doesn't run out. I found this horseshoe wall hook on eBay for $4. It's pretty heavy, so we secured it to the wall with mounts.

Out West, you can rustle up real tumbleweed for an authentic still life. If you can't find any tumbleweed where you live, tie a bunch of twigs together with some rope for a similar look.

I cracked up when I found this bed—to me, it looked like a little Western jail cell. This extendable bed will expand to an adult twin size as Makhi gets older. The wooden trunk was a salvage-yard find. We cleaned it up and now it makes a rustic toy box. To avoid smashed fingers, we installed a child safety lock and locking arms to keep the lid in place when open or shut.

Woolen Mexican blankets make a colorful bed cover and window dressing. The window treatment was made by running a straight stitch down one edge of the blanket to form a channel. A tension rod was run through the channel and wedged into the window jamb.

Additional wall hooks are handy storage for a cowpoke's gear. On the walls is a faux denim paint treatment. (Get details on page 164.)

the project

COVERED LAMP

Giving plain table lamps some Western flair has never been easier. Faux suede fringe and upholstery tack trim can be found inexpensively in the notions department of any fabric store and will make quite an impression. So pull your glue gun from its holster and get ready for a showdown.

Items you will need:

Lamp with shade

Cowhide fabric

Spray adhesive

Suede fringe trim

Hot-glue gun and glue sticks

Upholstery tack trim

Scissors

Here's how you do it:

1. First, cut the cow fabric to size and adhere to the lamp shade with the spray adhesive. Use the lamp shade as a template for your fabric.

2. Next, attach the suede fringe using the hot-glue gun.

3. Using the scissors, cut the upholstery tack trim to size and affix with the hot glue.

I added another touch by wrapping rope around the lamp's base and securing it with the hot glue.

c is for cole

THE NURSERY IS NOT SIMPLY A ROOM WHERE A BABY SLEEPS. THIS IS A magical, multipurpose space in the home where babies play, moms nurse, dads pace, big sisters read, and grandparents generally act pretty silly. Because everyone in the family will be doing their time in the nursery over the years, consider all their needs when designing these rooms:

- START FROM THE GROUND UP. The baby will spend a lot of time on the floor; ergo you will spend a lot of time on the floor. Take it easy on everybody's knees by investing in some cushy floor covering. Wall-to-wall is great, but if you have hardwood or vinyl floors, consider a low-pile shag area rug. You can purchase inexpensive, bound remnants at most carpeting stores.

- MAKE IT SAFE. Tall bookcases are a great storage solution for books, bears, and clothing, but they can tumble down onto curious climbers. Talk to a professional at your local hardware or children's furnishings stores about tethers

and straps to keep your tall furnishings against the wall where they belong.

- AMPLE SEATING FOR, UM, *AMPLE* BEHINDS. A while back, I bought my daughter a tea table with four tiny little chairs. Sure, they're the perfect size for her and her playdate cronies. But I felt like Goldilocks, about to break through Baby Bear's chair, whenever I would gingerly perch on one. I remedied the situation by replacing two of the four petite chairs with adult-sized wicker ottomans. The romantic style of the ottomans blends nicely with the princess decor in the room, their low profile allows them to be tucked under the table when not in use, and their generous landing pad allows Mom and Dad to enjoy the party, too. The moral of this story is: The seating in your child's room should not be "too hard, too soft, or too small, but just right" for everybody.

the dilemma

The morning sickness has come and gone, and the baby showers are over. All our parents-to-be need now is the baby and a little personality for his nursery. Mom and Dad have stashed the booty from the parade of showers in a spare bedroom that will soon be home to Baby Cole, but they would like to see a cozier, more inviting space. The challenge is where to start. They have all the necessities, but the room remains cold and unfinished. Pulling this room together in time for the new arrival will be my job.

THE GOOD NEWS

- All major furnishings have been purchased, leaving the majority of my budget for fun things.
- The ceilings are 9 feet high, and the room is relatively spacious for a city home (12 by 14 feet).
- The carpet is in excellent condition due to a no-shoe rule imposed by Mom and Dad since they moved in four years earlier (this is a great rule to have with little ones crawling around).

THE BAD NEWS

- There is no place to change the baby.
- The closet has no doors.
- The current color palette is bland and uninteresting.

THE PLAN

I want to make this a room that the whole family can enjoy by introducing four elements: color, work surfaces, lighting, and storage. All of these components are equally important for a successful nursery, and I plan to do it all for less than $500.

THE GRAND TOTAL: $467.90

AFTER

BEFORE

the color palette

The color scheme for this room is a traditional blue for boys. Cole's mom had already purchased stunning smoky blue and cream bedding for the crib, which made my job a lot easier. When choosing a color scheme for any room, start with textiles. Paint is the most versatile element and the easiest to change, so save that decision till the end to ensure the most harmonious look. If you still have trouble finding a perfect match, most paint companies provide a color-matching service. Bring in anything: a swatch of fabric, a photo from a magazine, even a favorite sweater.

NEW USES: **KITCHEN ACCESSORIES**

Changing a baby can be like wrestling an angry, greased piglet. This is a job you want done efficiently and fast, and digging around for lotions and creams will have your little piggy a-squealin' and you reaching for the Tylenol. I wanted to create a handy depository for Cole's parents, a spot for them to store the little particulars they will need each and every time that little bottom gets wiped. What did the trick were kitchen utensil holders. This iron rack with its steel cup attachments was meant to hold forks and spoons above a countertop. The size of the cups was perfect for creams and thermometers, while the color and arrangement worked nicely with my design. When searching for organizational tools for your own home, don't limit yourself. Every department in a home store has an organizational section. Don't even read the labels—it'll just confuse you; simply look at the items individually to find a perfect match for your unique storage challenges.

CONVERTIBLE NURSERY FURNITURE

It's a good idea to choose nursery furnishings that will grow with your child. Babies grow up fast, some faster than others, and you don't want to be stuck with a $1,400 crib that you can't use after the first year. The changing table I purchased for Cole's room is convertible. Once the days of dirty diapers have come and gone, the tabletop can be removed and the unit used as a chest of drawers.

Many companies also offer cribs that convert into toddler beds, and some models even morph into full-sized adult beds after that. If you make the right purchase now, you may need to buy only one bed for your child until he moves off and gets married (his wife will be making the decorating decisions from there on out—sorry, Mom).

the details

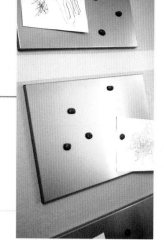

Bulletin boards are fun ways to display children's artwork. I purchased three stainless-steel boards and hung them in a row to form an entire wall, just waiting for little Cole to start scribbling. (See how the river-rock magnets were made on page 177.)

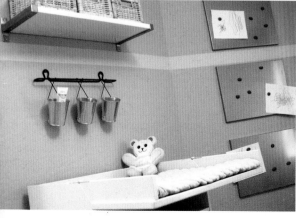

Changing diapers is a big part of any new mom's job. I set up a changing station in this nursery, fully equipped with changing pad, baskets for storage, and small containers for creams and lotions. (These containers had another original use; see what they were meant for on page 173.)

Storage and seating are combined with this cute wooden bench. The unfinished piece was painted a dark, smoky blue to coordinate with the rest of the room. Casters were attached to its base for added height and mobility, and Cole can keep his toys in the baskets.

The white cotton drapery panels in the nursery were nice but plain. To add some interest, I attached blue-and-white gingham ribbon to the panels using iron-on hem tape. (For step-by-step instructions, see Monogrammed Pillow on page 18.)

Cole's closet space had no doors and was open for the world to see. We disguised the clutter by hanging curtains. I went to my local window and blind shop and purchased ceiling curtain tracks (you may remember these from the hospital). The tracks are screwed into the ceiling and come with drapery clips that slide into the track and hold the curtain panels in place. This is an easy and inexpensive way to build a closet, or section off areas in your home.

the projects

C IS FOR COLE

Painting simple murals on a child's wall is a creative way to add a personal touch. The advantage paint has over wallpaper or other adhesive material is that once the child has outgrown the look, removal is simple; you just paint right over it. My inspiration for the mural's design was vintage alphabet books—you know, "A is for Apple," "B is for Boat," et cetera. You can project the image onto your wall using an overhead projector (these can be rented from certain camera shops or libraries), but I used carbon paper (remember carbon paper?).

Items you will need:

Image

Carbon paper

Painter's tape

Pencil

2 shades of blue paint, 1 a shade lighter than the other

Artist's brushes

Here's how you do it:

1. Acquire the image. I typed mine on the computer and took the print to the copy shop, where they enlarged it to epic proportions.

2. Paint the room with the darker shade of blue and allow it to dry.

3. Next, place the carbon paper on the wall, and place the image on top. Secure with the painter's tape and trace the image onto the wall with the pencil.

4. The last step is to fill in the image with the lighter blue paint with the artist's brush.

   If you're feeling good about your artistry, you can move on to more advanced projects like the monkeys we painted in this room. It's the same process; we just had an image of a monkey enlarged at the copy shop.

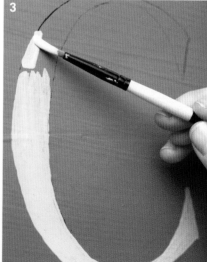

RIVER-ROCK MAGNETS

For a special touch, I decided to customize some ordinary round magnets for Cole's bulletin boards. In the mosaic tile section of my local craft store, I found the cutest little rocks with words carved into the surface such as JOY, HOPE, LAUGHTER, and HUGS. Since the synthetic rocks were designed for mosaics, their backs are flat and perfect to adhere to the flat surface of the magnets. Small tiles of any sort would work for this project.

Items you will need:

Mosaic rocks

Hot-glue gun and glue sticks

Flat, round magnets

Here's how you do it:

1. First, add a small dab of the glue to the back of the mosaic tile or stone.

2. Next, attach the magnet. Hold the magnet in place until the glue dries.

flower power

BUT, MOMMMMM . . . THE KEY TO SUCCESS WHEN REDECORATING A TEEN-ager's room is compromise. Let's face it, with a few exceptions, they all think we're square, and we all think they're kooky. Finding a middle ground will leave the kids feeling cool and us not having to close the room off every time our friends come to visit.

- **"BUT JUSTIN IS SO DREAMY. . . ."** Teenagers must have posters in their room; I think it's the law. If the look of tattered, tacked-up posters is simply more than you can handle, consider having them matted and framed. Arrange the frames in an organized, stylish manner and you have an easy compromise. Choose frames with removable backs, so when the next boy band hits, you can easily change the "art."

- **CONSIDER SEATING.** Your teenager is bound to have his buddies over from time to time. Invest in some funky, inexpensive seating such as beanbags or benches. A bench with storage under the seat is a double winner.

- **HAVE AN OPEN MIND.** The teenage years are a wonderful time in children's lives—a time for figuring out who they are and expressing themselves through their clothes, their music, and their room. Try to cut them some slack. It's just a room, after all, and you can always repaint when they're off at college.

the dilemma

Kelly is a popular, energetic fourteen-year-old. She excels at sports and does well in school. While Kelly is at camp, her sweet mother would like to treat her daughter to a surprise bedroom makeover as a reward for all her hard work. The teenager has apparently expressed some dissatisfaction in the room's general lack of "coolness," and would like to see a more hip, sophisticated look in her room. Mom would like to see "cool, but tame": no zebra-print wallpaper and fur-covered dressers in this house, thank you very much. I'm certain we can come up with a design that will make everyone happy before Kelly gets back.

THE GOOD NEWS

- The room is large (15 by 14 feet).
- The neutral low-pile shag is clean and will blend with any decor.
- The beautiful French doors open onto a private, second-floor deck; privacy is not a major concern.

THE BAD NEWS

- The beige-on-beige color scheme is drab.
- The furnishings are somewhat old-fashioned for a teenager.
- The bedding and curtains are dated and cannot be salvaged for my design.

THE PLAN

Kelly is still a young girl; I want to avoid designing a look that is too grown-up. She needs a room that has a touch of glam and sophistication but still represents her youth and individuality. I plan to remove most of the children's items but retain those that still have personal meaning to the fourteen-year-old. New fabrics and accessories will be introduced that have more color and

AFTER

BEFORE

excitement but still a youthful feel. I will bring in new lighting, more seating, and a fresh, hip look—all for less than $500.

THE GRAND TOTAL: $481.42

the color palette

Almost everything in Kelly's bedroom was the same pink-beige color—the walls, the carpet, the bedding, even the furniture had a creamy, rose hue. The only other "color" in the room was white, and that doesn't count. The lack of contrast and interest in this room was leaving Kelly feeling blue. Her mom couldn't figure out how to initiate change, so she called me. I didn't want to splash the room in color because the rest of the home is tastefully decorated in a soft neutral palette, and I didn't want this room to stand

out like a sore thumb. I needed only to add the right tones in the right values to spruce up this space.

On the first day of shopping, I found this lovely floral tapestry and immediately knew it would be perfect for Kelly. The pale pink flowers complement the existing furniture, while the fuchsia, sage, and black tones add punch to the bland bedding. I pulled the green tones from the tapestry onto the walls with paint, and scattered black accents throughout the room to bring balance to the space.

PAINT COLOR
Hillsmere, Kelly-Moore KM3411-1

NEW USES: **THE TROUBLE WITH TRIVETS**

Necessity is often the mother of my invention. (To be honest, the majority of the repurposed items in this book were actually born out of sheer desperation; $500 is not a lot of money.) However, sometimes it's different. One afternoon while shopping in the kitchenwares section of IKEA, I stumbled upon an enormous stack of round cork trivets they were selling for *only $1 each*. (If you are unfamiliar with them, trivets keep hot pots and pans from scorching your countertops.) I had absolutely no idea what I could use these for, but they were only *$1* for cryin' out loud. Soooo . . . I bought one hundred. I

sat on those babies for months trying to figure out a good use for them. Until I met Kelly (cue the singing angels), who needed architectural interest and a new corkboard. Voilà! We had a match. I filled the back of my truck with these little gems and nailed them all over her wall. They make a bold graphic statement, and Kelly can even hang her posters there. If you have time while shopping, take a moment to study the sizes, shapes, and textures of the items you see. You may find a repurposing prospect yourself.

SHORT-TERM DECOR

Kelly is a trendy teenager, and like all trendy teenagers she wanted only the *most fabulous* colors for her room. Hot pink was all the rage that week, but I felt that she and her family would be happier with colors that would stand the test of time. We settled on a more neutral green tone for the walls. The furnishings were left their original creamy hue, and black accents were brought in for interest. But I couldn't let Kelly down: She wanted some hot color. So a blast of color came with the new bed throw and interchangeable accents such as pillows and art. These less expensive pieces can be replaced should Kelly change her style.

When decorating your child's room, remember how fickle she can be (especially a teenager). Do yourself a favor and keep the major components of the room basic. Pottery Barn Teen has a wonderful selection of relatively inexpensive beds, nightstands, and desks that are hip but will stand the test of time. Then get crazy with the details. If she insists on some bright colors for her walls, consider a single accent wall, which will be much easier to repaint when the day comes. As for accessories, Urban Outfitters has the most unique inventory of trendy clothing and home accessories I have found. The items are relatively inexpensive and sure to please the fashionista in your own home.

the details

Kelly's mom told me that the one thing Kelly would especially want changed were the curtains: She disliked their old-fashioned appearance. I exchanged the old, floral draperies for simple cream cotton panels and peachy keen sheers.

A large, rectangular mirror replaces the dinky bulletin board Kelly had over the desk. The scale of the mirror works better in the room, and the silverleaf detail adds a touch of sophistication. Interest is added with a sleek, black desk chair.

Kelly's old desk chair is now a nice landing spot for clothes or extra seating when friends visit. We made the floral lamp shades ourselves using hot glue and bridal flowers. (Find out how on page 185.)

A simple framed print coordinates with the new floral bedding. The graphic wall design is actually a wall-sized corkboard made from kitchen trivets. (Get details on page 184.)

Kelly's mom was not about to let me paint the bed (I had to ask)—it's a family heirloom, and she watched me closely whenever I went near it. To give the antique a fresher appearance, I decided to disguise it instead. This linen cover was purchased in a standard, full size from IKEA ($40). It slipped right over the French Provincial headboard—no alterations needed. The bed now has a more modern sleek line, but Mom can rest easy.

the projects

CORK HEADBOARD

This impressive structure behind Kelly's bed is a collection of cork kitchen trivets. They make a bold graphic statement in the room, were cheap at $1 apiece (IKEA), and can double as a bulletin board for posters of guys in boy bands.

Items you will need:

Measuring tape

Pencil

Trivets: I used 100 and saved money by not putting any behind the bed

Finishing nails

Hammer

Level

Here's how you do it:

1. Using the measuring tape, measure the width you would like the board to be, and mark each side with the pencil. Place the first trivet in the bottom left corner and attach it to the wall with the finishing nail right through the center.

2. Begin to work to your right, using the level to ensure everything is even.

3. Once the bottom row is finished, begin working upward until you've formed an L shape. Now you can simply fill in the rest of the trivets knowing the grid will be uniform.

FLOWER LAMP

To add an ultrafeminine touch to any lamp shade, all you need are a ton of flowers and some hot glue. These flowers can be purchased at any fabric or craft store. I purchased white silk roses in bulk from eBay. Just type "white silk roses" in the search field and thousands of options appear. These particular flowers were sold from a bridal company and were really inexpensive—I bought two hundred for $39.

Items you will need:

Silk roses: approximately 45 to 60 for an average-sized lamp shade

Scissors

Hot-glue gun and glue sticks

Lamp shade

Here's how you do it:

1. The silk flowers usually come on stems. Remove the blossoms from the stems and clip off the extra greenery at the base of the flower. You want the flower to lie flush onto the lamp shade.

2. Add a generous dab of hot glue to the base of the flower.

3. Attach the flowers to the lamp shade, firmly pressing them down until the glue has dried.

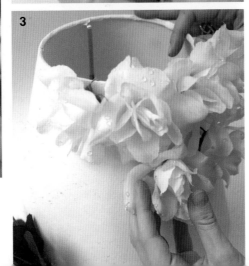

resources

FURNISHINGS

Design Within Reach
(800) 944-2233
www.dwr.com

Ethan Allen
(888) EAHELP1 (324-3571)
www.ethanallen.com

IKEA
www.ikea.com

Pottery Barn
(888) 779-5176
www.potterybarn.com

Pottery Barn Teen
(866) 472-4001
www.potterybarnteen.com

Scandinavian Designs, Inc.
www.scandinaviandesigns.com

Smith & Hawken
(800) 940-1170
www.smithandhawken.com

PAINT, BRUSHES, AND PAINT SERVICES

Brescia-Stone Painting, Inc.
(415) 898-0388
www.bresciastonepainting.com

Color Your World Faux Finishing
(650) 703-8728
(510) 530-1120

Gardner's Paint and Faux Finish
(707) 557-5940

Kelly-Moore Paints
www.kellymoore.com

Purdy Products
(503) 286-8217
www.purdycorp.com

FABRIC AND ACCESSORIES

Bed Bath and Beyond, Inc.
(800) GOBEYOND (462-3966)
www.bedbathandbeyond.com

Discount Fabrics
3006 San Pablo Avenue
Berkeley, CA 94702
(510) 548-2981

eBay
www.ebay.com

El Paso Import Co.
(888) 999-3773
www.elpasoimportco.com

JOE BOXER
www.joeboxer.com

Michaels Stores, Inc.
(800) MICHAELS (642-4235)
www.michaels.com

Ohmega Salvage
2407 San Pablo Avenue
Berkeley, CA 94702
(510) 843-7368
www.ohmegasalvage.com

Orchard Supply Hardware
(888) SHOPOSH (746-7674)
www.osh.com

Pier 1 Imports
(800) 245-4595
www.pier1.com

Poppy Fabrics
5151 Broadway
Oakland, CA 94611-4619
(510) 655-5151

Stitch Lounge
182 Gough Street
San Francisco, CA 94102-5918
(415) 431-3SEW (3739)
www.stitchlounge.com
Target
(800) 440-0680
www.target.com

Urban Ore Building Materials
900 Murray Street
Berkeley, CA 94710
(510) 841-SAVE (7283)

Urban Outfitters
(800) 959-8794
www.urbanoutfitters.com

Z Gallerie
(800) 358-8288
www.zgallerie.com

index

a

African Lounge, 128–135
    the color palette, 130–131
    the details, 132–133
    the dilemma, 130
    the projects, 134–135
Altars, 123, 125
Area rug headboards, 15, 16, 19
Armoires, 140, 142–143
Artificial flower arrangements, 147
Artwork
    backdrops for framed art, 91
    botanical prints, 66, 69
    Burger King crown stencil, 118
    chalkboard art, 93
    frames as, 47
    geometric shapes painted on walls, 105
    internationally inspired fabric, 133
    maps, framed, 99
    mouse pads affixed to wall, 22
    murals, 176
    packaging labels as, 165
    place mat art, 109
    pop art self-portraits, 57, 58
    posters, 124, 128, 178
    rubber-stamp art, 47
    scale concerns, 115, 124
    sculptures, 140, 147
    smaller pieces presented in uniform fashion, 105
    tin ceiling tiles used for, 157
    tribal mask art, 132, 134
    wall art, 82, 85
    wall clocks, 107, 108
Asian Retreat, 136–143
    the color palette, 138–139
    the details, 140–141
    the dilemma, 138
    the project, 142–143

b

Bamboo, potted, 99
Bamboo gardening stakes, 91
Bars, 91, 131
Baskets, 39
Beams, painting of, 126
Bedding, 74
Bedrooms
    office equipment in, 15
    reading spaces in, 17, 70
    See also Asian Retreat; Children's rooms; Gothic
        Bedroom; Pad Thai; Peaceful Bedroom; Pop
        Art Bedroom; Sexy Bedroom
Beer buckets, 123
Benches, 175
Bird feeders, 56
Blackout curtains, 12
Blinds, 80
Bolster pillows, 49
Bookshelves, 83
Botanical Dining Room, 62–69

the color palette, 65
    the details, 66–67
    the dilemma, 64
    the projects, 68–69
Botanical prints, 66, 69
Buffet lamps, 106
Bulletin boards
    for nurseries, 174, 177
    for office spaces, 83, 84
Burger King crown stencil, 118
Burger King crown window treatments, 119
Butcher block islands, 131

c

Candleholders, 32, 67
Candles, 74, 116, 141
Canopies, 148, 151
Ceiling curtain tracks, 175
Ceilings
    painted beams, 126
    starry ceiling, 35
Ceiling tile headboards, 150
Chairs
    outdoor furniture, 32, 97
    as plant stands, 149
    plastic-and-aluminum dining chairs, 106
    retro aluminum chairs, 82
    rocking chairs, 159
    wicker chairs, 124
Chalkboard art, 93
Chandelier accents, 98–99
Changing stations, 174
Chests of drawers, 82
Children's rooms
    short-term decor for, 181
    See also C Is for Cole; Cowpoke Nursery;
        Flower Power; Pretty in Pink Nursery
C Is for Cole (nursery), 170–177
    the color palette, 172–173
    the details, 174–175
    the dilemma, 172
    the projects, 176–177
Clocks, 107, 108
Coffee tables, 25, 133
Computer hutches, 62
Consignment stores, 81
Console tables, 24
Contemporary Dining Room, 102–109
    the color palette, 104–105
    the details, 106–107
    the dilemma, 104
    the projects, 108–109
Convertible nursery furniture, 173
Cork headboards, 181, 183, 184
Cowpoke Nursery, 162–169
    the color palette, 164–165
    the details, 166–167
    the dilemma, 164
    the project, 168–169
Crystal prisms for light fixtures, 31
Curtains. *See* Window treatments

d

Denim paint treatment, 164, 167
Dens. *See* African Lounge; Moroccan Den
Dining rooms
    reading spaces in, 41
    storage in, 62
    See also Botanical Dining Room; Contemporary
      Dining Room; Feminine Dining Room
Dining tables, 107
Dinnerware, 40
Dog beds, 47
Doors used at tabletops, 115, 116
Drapery headboards, 51
Drapes. *See* Window treatments
Dressers, 158
Dying of fabrics, 73

e

Entertainment centers, 70
Epoxy paint, 140

f

Feminine Dining Room, 36–43
    the color palette, 39
    the details, 40–41
    the dilemma, 38
    the projects, 42–43
Finials, rope, 76
Fireplace covers, 24, 26
Fireplaces
    natural elements for, 23, 41
    pressed tin fireplace, 127
Floor coverings
    faux slate floor, 99, 101
    for nurseries, 157
    zebra rugs, 17
Floor screens as wall hangings, 117
Floral Workspace, 78–85
    the color palette, 81
    the details, 82–83
    the dilemma, 80
    the projects, 84–85
Flower lamp, 185
Flower Power (teenager's room), 178–185
    the color palette, 180–181
    the details, 182–183
    the dilemma, 180
    the projects, 184–185
Flowers. *See* Natural elements
Fountains, 98, 100
Frames as artworks, 47
Futons, 78, 83, 117

g

Gargoyle lamps, 48, 50
Gingham ribbon, 158, 175
Gold-leafing, 142–143
Gothic Bedroom, 44–51
    the color palette, 47
    the details, 48–49
    the dilemma, 45
    the projects, 50–51
Greenhouse accessories, 107
Guest room/office combo. *See* Floral Workspace

h

Hawaiian lamp shade, 24, 27
Headboards
    area rug headboards, 15, 16, 19
    ceiling tile headboards, 150
    cork headboards, 181, 183, 184
    drapery headboards, 51
    faux headboards, 141
    linen covers for, 183
    pillow headboards, 59
    pot rack headboards, 33, 34
    tufted headboards, 75, 76–77
Home offices. *See* Office spaces
Hooks on walls, 32, 149
Horseshoe wall hooks, 166

i

Interior designers, 120
Internet shopping, 165

j

Jade Living Room, 86–93
    the color palette, 88–89
    the details, 90–92
    the dilemma, 88
    the project, 93

k

Kitchen utensil holders, 173

l

Lamps. *See* Lighting
Lamp shades
    for chandeliers and sconces, 42
    flower lamp, 185
    Hawaiian lamp shade, 24, 27
    looped fringes for, 75
    tutu lamp shades, 158, 161
    Western lamp shades, 168–169
    wicker lamp shades, 66
Lanterns, 66, 132
Laundry bins, 56
Lemon scent, 116
Leopard print fabric, 124
Lighting
    buffet lamps, 106
    candles, 74, 116, 141
    chandelier accents, 98–99
    crystal prisms for fixtures, 31
    desk lamps mounted to walls, 16
    faux crystal chandeliers, 49
    gargoyle lamps, 48, 50
    lanterns, 66, 132
    picture light used as reading light, 148
    pot racks for overhead lighting, 90, 92
    wall sconces, 148
    See also Lamp shades
Living rooms. *See* Jade Living Room;
    Mexican Living Room
Luxe Patio, 94–101
    the color palette, 96–97
    the details, 98–99
    the dilemma, 96
    the projects, 100–101

m

Magnets, river-rock, 174, 177
Maps, framed, 99
Mattresses, 70
Message centers, 67, 68
Mexican blankets, 167
Mexican Living Room, 120–127
   the color palette, 123
   the details, 124–125
   the dilemma, 122
   the projects, 126–127
Mirrors, 41, 48, 141, 182
Monogrammed pillows, 16, 18
Moroccan Den, 112–119
   the color palette, 115
   the details, 116–117
   the dilemma, 114
   the projects, 118–119
Moulin Rouge Studio, 28–35
   the color palette, 31
   the details, 32–33
   the dilemma, 30
   the projects, 34–35
Mouse pads affixed to wall, 22
Movie posters, 124
Murals, 176

n

Natural elements
   artificial flower arrangements, 147
   bamboo, potted, 99
   bamboo gardening stakes, 91
   botanical prints, 66, 69
   for fireplaces, 23, 41
   lemon scent, 116
   long-stemmed roses, 32
   nature-scape planter, 135
   plant stands, 147, 149
   sources of outdoor decor, 65
   teddy bear topiary, 159, 160
   tumbleweed, 166
Nightstands, 75
Night tables, 17
Nudie posters, 128
Nurseries
   convertible furniture for, 173
   floor coverings for, 157
   storage in, 154
   See also C Is for Cole;
      Cowpoke Nursery;
      Pretty in Pink Nursery

o

Office spaces
   bedrooms used for, 15
   computer hutches for, 62
   office/guest room combos.
      See Floral Workspace
   reading spaces in, 25
   See also Surfer Chic Lounge
Organization racks, 159
Outdoor furniture, 32, 97

p

Packaging labels, 165
Pad Thai, 144–151
   the color palette, 146–147
   the details, 148–149
   the dilemma, 146
   the projects, 150–151
Painting tips, 86, 89
Paper
   with Japanese designs, 139
   wrapping paper, 39, 42, 43
Patios. See Luxe Patio
Peaceful Bedroom, 70–77
   the color palette, 72–73
   the details, 74–75
   the dilemma, 72
   the projects, 76–77
Pillow headboards, 59
Pillows
   animal prints for, 57
   bolster pillows, 49
   decorative accents for, 82
   monogrammed pillows, 16, 18
   for Moroccan ambiance, 117
   as seating, 116
   throw pillows, 90
Place mat art, 109
Place mats, 43
Plants. See Natural elements
Pop Art Bedroom, 52–60
   the color palette, 55
   the details, 56–57
   the dilemma, 54
   the projects, 58–59
Pop art self-portraits, 57, 58
Posters, 124, 128, 178
Pot rack headboards, 33, 34
Pot racks for overhead lighting, 90, 92
Pre-owned furnishings, 162
Pretty in Pink Nursery, 154–161
   the color palette, 156–157
   the details, 158–159
   the dilemma, 156
   the projects, 160–161
Projects
   area rug headboard, 19
   botanical prints, 69
   Burger King crown stencil, 118
   Burger King crown window treatments, 119
   canopy, 151
   ceiling tile headboard, 150
   chalkboard art, 93
   cork headboard, 184
   drapery headboard, 51
   faux slate floor, 101
   fireplace cover, 26
   flower lamp, 185
   fountain, 100
   gargoyle lamps, 50
   gold-leafing, 142–143
   Hawaiian lamp shade, 27
   lamp shades for chandeliers and sconces, 42
   magnetic bulletin board, 84
   message center, 68

monogrammed pillow, 18
murals, 176
nature-scape planter, 135
painted beams, 126
pillow headboard, 59
place mat art, 109
place mats, 43
pop art self-portrait, 58
pot rack headboard, 34
pressed tin fireplace, 127
river-rock magnets, 177
rope finials, 76
starry ceiling, 35
teddy bear topiary, 160
tribal mask art, 134
tufted headboard, 76–77
tutu lamp shades, 161
wall art, 85
wall clock, 108
Western lamp, 168–169

r

Reading spaces
    in bedrooms, 17, 70
    in dining rooms, 41
    in home offices, 25
River-rock magnets, 174, 177
Rocking chairs, 159
Rose petals, 49
Roses, long-stemmed, 32
Rubber-stamp art, 47
Rugs. See Floor coverings

S

Sculptures, 140, 147
Sectioning off areas of the home, 175
Sexy Bedroom, 12–19
    the color palette, 15
    the details, 16–17
    the dilemma, 14
    the projects, 18–19
Shelving
    for books, 83
    greenhouse accessories on, 107
    as night tables, 17
Shower-curtain liners, 32, 80
Shower curtains, 40
Sideboards, 105
Sofas, 25, 117
Sofa tables, 24
Starry ceiling, 35
Storage
    armoires, 140, 142–143
    baskets, 39
    in dining rooms, 62
    dressers, 158
    kitchen utensil holders, 173
    laundry bins, 56
    nightstands, 75
    in nurseries, 154
    organization racks, 159
    professional help for storage problems, 20
    toy boxes, 166
    wall hooks, 32, 149
    wooden benches used for, 175

Studio apartments. See Moulin Rouge Studio
Surfer Chic Lounge, 20–27
    the color palette, 23
    the details, 24–25
    the dilemma, 22
    the projects, 26–27

t

Table runners, 67
Tables
    coffee tables, 25, 133
    dining tables, 107
    doors used at tabletops, 115, 116
    glass-topped tables, 98
    night tables, 17
    outdoor furniture, 32, 97
    sofa (console) tables, 24
Tapestries, 149
    as window treatments, 133
Teddy bear topiary, 159, 160
Throw pillows, 90
Tile work, faux, 116
Tin ceiling tiles, 157
Topiary project, 160
Toy boxes, 166
Tribal mask art, 132, 134
Trivets, 181, 183, 184
Tufted headboards, 75, 76–77
Tumbleweed, 166
Tutu lamp shades, 158, 161

U

"Use what you have" consultation services, 120

V

Vanities, 139

W

Wall art, 82, 85
Wall sconces, 148
Western lamps, 168–169
Wicker chairs, 124
Wicker lamp shades, 66
Windows in odd shapes and sizes, 55
Window treatments
    blackout curtains, 12
    blinds, 80
    Burger King crown window treatments, 119
    canvas draperies, 149
    cotton panels, 182
    gingham ribbon for, 158, 175
    Mexican blankets, 167
    rope finials, 76
    sheers, 149, 182
    shower-curtain liners, 32, 80
    shower curtains, 40
    tapestries, 133
Wineglasses as candleholders, 32
Wrapping paper, 39, 42, 43

Z

Zebra rugs, 17